Biz 4.0

By Ade McCormack

The Digital Strategy series:

The IT Value Stack – A Boardroom Guide to IT Leadership

IT Demystified – The IT handbook for Digital Leaders

Biz 4.0 – An Anthropological Blueprint for Business in the Digital Age

The Digital Life series:

Attention Dynamics: High Personal Performance in the Digital Age

Beyond Nine to Five: Your Career Guide for the Digital Age

Also by Ade:

The e-Skills Manifesto: A Call to Arms *

This book is available as a FREE PDF download from

www.ademccormack.com

where you can also access Ade's blogs

Digital Life

Digital Strategy

Biz 4.0

An anthropological blueprint for business in the Digital Age

First edition

Ade McCormack

Published by Auridian Press
www.auridian.com
Enquires: info@auridian.com

First published in Great Britain in 2017. Issue 1.0

ISBN 978-0954765156

British Library Cataloguing in Publication Data

A CIP catalogue record for this book can be obtained from the British Library

Auridian Press is a division of Auridian Consulting Ltd.

Dedication

This book is dedicated to tribal leaders, past, present and future.

Contents

Table of figures

Preface

The following companies are part of a not so-exclusive club, where the admission criterion is simply to have presumed the past was an indicator of the future. Consequently, they pursued a strategy that became increasingly decoupled from reality:

- Nokia – Didn't see the smartphone coming.
- DEC (Digital Equipment Corp) – Didn't see the PC coming.
- Blockbuster – Failed to recognise how lazy its customers were.
- ICL – Thought there was only a market for mainframes.
- Marconi – 'Bet the farm' on telecoms infrastructure.
- Borders – Chose physical over digital.
- Commodore Corp – Didn't embrace the PC architecture.
- Palm – Out-innovated by Apple.
- Kodak – Digital inertia.

There are more companies that whilst not gaining admittance to this club are today operating as shadows of their former selves. Even more have had near death experiences, but through luck or judgement have been able to pull out of their nosedive, or at least they have softened the angle of descent. Such descents can be attributed to many factors, including poor management, over leverage, drop in demand, and challenger upstarts. But perhaps the underlying cause was that they failed to detect these problems in time to do something, perhaps even something radical, to address them.

One of the problems corporations face today is that the clock-speed of business is accelerating, so the mean time between problem detection and 'game over' is shrinking rapidly. But then there is also the matter of market uncertainty. We are indeed living in uncertain times.

Car makers can no longer model with any accuracy the future demand for cars. Similarly, hotel chains cannot be certain that growing their property portfolio is the best way forward. Smartphone manufacturers cannot be certain that they will be able to acquire the raw materials they need to meet likely ongoing market demand.

Consequently, strategy and strategic planning is becoming more real-time in nature. Strategy has morphed from 'let's build a few pyramids over the next few years', with the confidence that the materials and labour are readily available, to being more akin to a hyper-vigilant, anxiety-rich fighter jet pilot in the midst of a dog fight. Only the very foolish would make big bets on the future.

But the truth is that we have always lived in uncertain times. The risk of starvation or death by consumption was a daily reality for our ancestors. Our forefathers lived in a world where there was a real danger that 'lunch' might well turn on its prospective diners mid-hunt. It is only in the last couple of centuries that mankind has attempted to engineer certainty into our existence.

Most notably, at least for first world nations, a sense of safety, and abundance in respect of food. In fact, courtesy of the industrial era, we structured our existence to the point that we generally didn't need others to make our way through life. Supermarkets provided our food, and the military and emergency services handled our safety concerns. This sense of certainty also made it easier to anticipate demand, and thus invest capital in producing goods that were likely to be needed for an extended period beyond the building of the factory.

So, it might be more accurate to state that 'we are again living in uncertain times'. Many organisations are ignoring this, and are in effect 'dead men walking' because their only way to eke a profit is to focus on increasing operational efficiency.

Similarly, consumers continue to buffer the growing disparity between their earnings expectations and their sliding market value by the use of credit. For many, this is the equivalent of the final days of the Roman empire. The growth in populism is another indicator of our return to uncertainty.

MBA case studies are littered with examples of organisations that failed to adjust. We now live in a world where it is not inconceivable that the likes of AirBnB, Uber and Twitter will join the above list. It could be that on this very day, someone somewhere has abandoned their degree course to set up a new company which in due course will take out Google.

But the good news is that we are wired for uncertainty. Approximately one hundred percent of mankind's existence has been as a hunter gatherer, exposed to the malevolent realities of nature. The Industrial era, as we will see, was a blip in our existence when we were at our most disconnected from our true nature. The agricultural era, as we will also see, leans much more towards our hunter gatherer existence than our denatured industrial existence.

Just as the world is undergoing radical change, so is the very nature of business. Again, increased volatility and uncertainty means that organisations need the attentiveness of a mid-air trapeze artist. I have written this book to provide you with a way forward in respect of navigating the unforgiving terrain of this competitive savanna. This is not new to us as a species, but for various reasons, not least the needs of the factory owner, we have veered into this existential industrial cul-de-sac.

Keep in mind that bigger is not always better. Smaller pack animals do take down their larger prey through numbers, agility and sociality. But they are not always successful, so this isn't necessarily a winning formula. Fintech start-ups, are stalking the big financial players. And like a scene on the savanna, the bigger animals are not squaring up for a fight, but are not rolling onto their backs either.

My point being that it is not simply a case of agile and collaborative versus big and slow. It is much more nuanced. GE and Rolls Royce are a couple of examples of how the big players have adapted to the digital era. If we cast our minds back to the early days of oil exploration. The players would simply burn off the gas entombed in the wells, considering it to be a useless byproduct of their search for oil. Today, they have turned that by-product into value. The likes of GE and Rolls Royce are now doing the same with the large 'data byproduct' that their offerings are generating.

The arrival of the digital age is not necessarily a mass extinction event for large established organisations. But it is no longer business as usual. Organisations that wake up to this, and reengineer accordingly, have a fighting chance of thriving in this post-industrial world. This book is both the wake-up call and the strategic road map.

Biz 4.0 is aimed primarily at those who are strategically influential, as the future of business lies in your hands. Workers, also known as, talent, artists, human resources, the precariat and personnel, will benefit from understanding how digital puts you in control, if you are willing to 'up your game'. You will also develop a feel for what good looks like from a talent engagement perspective, and why you, as talent, or a talented leader, may be feeling unnecessary tension, and unfulfillment in your organisation.

Business/digital transformation/change is not a new topic. It is a reality of this return to uncertainty. However, I have concerns that there are some sweeping assumptions being made that will not help business or society make the necessary leap. Industry 4.0 is a high-profile example of such a 'rogue beacon'.

But why should you listen to my perspective? I have worked for over three decades at the forefront of technological change, initially as a technologist, and more latterly as an advisor to business leaders. Through my writing activities as a columnist for both CIO magazine and the Financial Times, I have been exposed to many leaders dealing with business transformation. Having worked in over thirty countries, across many sectors, I have a broad sense of what works and what doesn't.

Watching organisations respond to market pressures by getting their people to simply work harder, or throwing all their resources into process re-engineering, is painful to watch. Similarly building a stockpile of new technology, or having the 'biggest' data, as a solution to fundamental inadequacies in their business model is similarly futile.

In respect of the blueprint, I have taken a model that has worked very well for hundreds of thousands of years, and contextualised it for an organisation whose primary role is to generate value.

My underlying hypothesis is that humans are integral to organisational value generation, as is new technology. Keep in mind that we are careering fast towards a world where humans will not be required to work, so this model may only have a few decades of mileage in it. Nonetheless, organisations looking to be in business in the near to medium future will find my model to be of relevance.

At the most abstract level, the Biz 4.0 blueprint has three areas of attention:

- Capital.
    - There are five sources.
- Success factors.
    - I have identified five main themes.
- Human drivers.
    - I have identified nine relevant anthropological drivers.

Structurally, I make the case for the Biz 4.0 blueprint, prior to introducing it. I then present the blueprint, and its primary moving parts. We will then dig a little deeper into the capital elements (value creators) of the model, followed by an exploration of the success factors as a collective whole. Next, we will become familiar with the anthropological drivers that are hardwired into our nature.

These drivers impact all aspects of business, from the manner in which organisations design services, right through to how the workplace is structured.

Having set the foundations, we will explore the success factors in more detail. Each of these has their own key areas of focus, which we need to understand, if we are to truly build organisations wired for success. In each case, we also explore the associated capital and human implications. Finally, we will look at the recommended next steps from both the perspective of a start-up and an established organisation. We will also address wider considerations that the model does not explicitly seem to address.

By reading this book, you will have a greater understanding of the prevailing forces that are driving today's business realities. You will also have a simple framework that will enable you to steer your organisation through the digital tempest.

I appreciate that I am teasing you somewhat by being vague in respect of detail - capital? success factors? anthropological drivers? But all will be revealed shortly. At this stage, I ask that you simply internalise the three sides of the Biz 4.0 triangle.

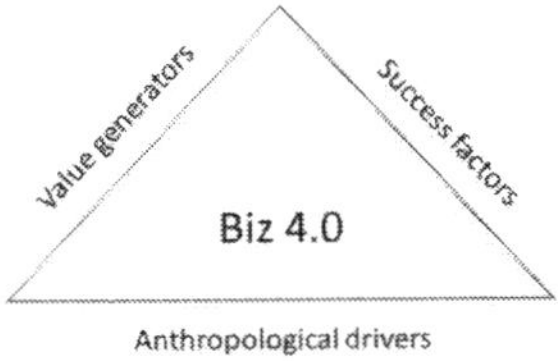

Figure 1 The Biz 4.0 triangle

As you read the book, I am sure many of you will have a sense of 'of course' in respect of the contents. Building businesses around our true nature is the essence of my message. Once we achieve that, then both going to work, and acquiring products and services, will resonate at a much deeper emotional level for both us and our people.

The industrial model edifice is crumbling. Businesses need to change. Biz 4.0 offers a model that embraces our natural, tried and tested, neurological wiring. It's time to make nature your business partner!

Ade McCormack, 2017

1 Making the case for change

Overview

In this chapter, we explore the changes that are forcing organisations to transform. By the end of this chapter, you will have a strong sense of whether your organisation is currently wired for the future, or for obsolescence.

Is your organisation built on an industrial era model?

A premise of Biz 4.0 is that the industrial era factory model is no longer fit for purpose as far as employees are concerned. A robot-driven factory with minimal human intervention has its place, for example in the production of vehicles, or the distribution of books. So, let us establish whether your organisation is in fact a factory. You might be fairly confident as to how this rough and ready test will play out for you. There are no conveyor belts in your organisation. Your people do not wear hard hats and boiler suits. So clearly you must be a post-industrial organisation. But bear with me for a second.

The first characteristic of an industrial era organisation is its emphasis on process, specifically the reengineering/refinement of its existing processes. This indicates a sense of market stability. Consequently, the focus is on maintaining that position through greater operational efficiency.

The second characteristic is the extent to which the leadership is centralised; strategic decision making is in the hands of a few individuals who spend much of their time in what is called a boardroom. The presumption is that everyone else in the organisation does not have a brain worth consulting, or is in fact employed on the understanding that they will not use their brain. Such is the nature of being a 'cog in the machine'.

The third characteristic, which relates to the first, is that there is a general belief that what made the organisation successful in the past will continue to make it successful into the future. Again, this relates to the industrial era notion of certainty.

Possibly, you now see your organisation in a different light?

The world is changing

We can say goodbye to certainty. Like our ancestors, we are living in an increasingly uncertain world. However, unlike our ancestors we have new communications technologies thrown into the mix. Thus, we are entering the era of hyper-uncertainty.

Political developments are redrawing alliances, and tensions. Whilst traditional warfare exists, cyber, media (fake news) and financial (currency exchange rate manipulation) warfare are now playing out on invisible battlefields.

Blue collar work continues to become automated. The emergence of the blue collarisation of white collar work, courtesy of new technologies, is causing the socially important middle class to fray in the developed world. Though at the same time, we are witnessing the creation of an emerging middle class in some major developing countries. As we will see, there is still a place for humans in the workplace, but these people will be the antithesis of the industrial era cog worker. Their scarcity, however, will cause the employer-employee power axis to lurch towards the employee.

Our rate of consumption of natural materials is unsustainable. As we are discovering, this is having an impact on both the fields of space exploration, and genetics.

Our enhanced interconnectedness has the effect of converting linear progressions into exponential explosions. A butterfly flapping its wings in the Philippines today will be a harnessed energy source tomorrow.

Business models are changing

As I have strongly alluded, the very nature of business is changing. A focus on process is giving way to a focus on innovation. And that innovation is increasingly data-driven in nature. Centralised leadership is giving way to decentralised leadership, enabling field operatives to respond to threats and opportunities in real-time, rather than after the next board meeting. And of course, certainty is being replaced by chaos. One cannot assume that the current drivers of success will be the future drivers.

Customers are increasingly fickle. Not only do they want value for little cost, or even for free, they want it with the minimal number of clicks, when and where it suits them. And not only must the product or service meet the stated functionality requirements, it must, in some cases, also confer a personal branding boost in the process, or at least make some sort of lifestyle statement. Increasingly customers are more interested in consumption than ownership, and this is upsetting the traditional sales process protocols.

The ensuing chaos of the market today means that organisations need to maintain a state of healthy paranoia about their business model's sustainability. As such, they need to be relentlessly exploring new offerings, and even new business models.

The nature of work is changing

In turn, the very nature of work is changing. People are reviewing their commitment to work in respect of the time they spend doing it compared to the level of satisfaction they receive. Funding affluent lifestyles to impress others, often with money they don't have does not appear to stack up.

People are reviewing what is important to them, and what they expect from their short stay on the planet, and the trend certainly isn't towards blind obedience to an organisation whose sole focus is on making shareholders wealthy.

The industrial model saw humans as a form of horsepower, and/or a technology placeholder. The technology is here now, so the demand for compliant process workers is diminishing fast. But there is a growing demand for people who can do things computers cannot do that are of value to the market. Such capability calls upon our creativity, and in turn our cognitive capacity to be creative. These rare people are calling the shots in terms of how they are engaged by corporations. The notion of a career for life is being replaced by a life of careers. Unlike their one-career predecessors, digital age talent is exploring multiple careers throughout their life, often running careers in parallel.

Talent management can no longer be solved by throwing money at the problem. Organisations need to create great workplaces that attract and retain the best talent, who as a group will work collaboratively to produce differentiated customer experiences. We are witnessing the transition of humans in the workplace from cogs to artists. This would appear to be a return to our tribal past. We want to be part of something that is going somewhere, and to be useful in the process.

We are wired to be hunter gatherers. So perhaps we are evolving into digital hunter gatherers? Digital in this case means augmented; the smartphone is the new spear. In any case, we want to operate in an environment where our innate curiosity is given free rein. The alternative is death by immobility and boredom. We appear to be returning to our tribal roots.

Defend, Disrupt or be disrupted

This human nature 'reset', coupled with increasing market volatility and technology evolution hitting the steep phase of the exponential growth curve, has created the perfect storm. Imagine a game, where not only are the goal posts moving, but the pitch is as well. On top of that, those that show signs of winning early on in the game get to write the rules for the rest of the game. In such conditions, there are really only three options. You can attempt to defend your territory by bracing for a market disruptor to attack. You can reinvent your organisation to be that disruptor. Or you can remain oblivious, hermetically-sealed from the digital-reality (an oxymoron?).

Business leaders can similarly be classified in this way. With that in mind, it is important to note that digital leadership is not a role, but a boardroom competence that all leaders need to acquire. The reality is that not only are most business leaders lacking this competence, they do not even have access to someone who can guide them in such matters. It is my view that this represents an opportunity for an ambitious Chief Information Officer (CIO), who recognises that the 'I' in CIO stands for information, and not IT (information technology). Similarly, Human Resource Directors (HRD), who see people less as 'resources', and more as humans, would have the foundations to lead the digital charge. In any case, having a digital executive in the leadership team would be a start. But keep in mind that the goal is for each member to be digitally competent.

This book was written to help business leaders on their journey to becoming digital business leaders, and thus equipping them to lead the ongoing transformation necessary to thrive in the digital age.

Take note

- Be clear on where your organisation is in respect of its journey towards digital-robustness. Being process-oriented, with a centralised leadership model, and a sense that the future will be similar to the past, albeit a little faster, would suggest that there is much work to be done.

- Whilst everything appears to be changing, the changing expectations of humans, particularly in respect of work and consumption, is where we need to place our attention.

- Whilst the objective in business is not to attack the competition, it is likely that if you are not out-innovating your competitors, in whatever form they take, you will likely be on the receiving end of the disruption transaction.

2 The Biz 4.0 blueprint

Overview

We have now established that there are seismic forces in play reshaping the world and the nature of business. The old strategic assumptions no longer hold true in this new era of volatility and uncertainty.

In this chapter, I provide an overview of the blueprint for a digital era business model. It can be thought of as a meta-strategy, in that it is identifying what needs to be considered in general terms, so that you can apply it to your specific situation.

We will explore the elements of the Biz 4.0 blueprint in detail in subsequent chapters. But first let us be clear by what we mean when we talk of transformation and digital.

Transformation?

Transformation has become a much-used term in respect of business strategy. We used to talk about change management, so is it just a modern reference to change?

Transformation might be considered 'extreme change'. The caterpillar grows, and so it changes. It becomes a butterfly. This is transformation.

The transition from the industrial era to the digital era is not a change, it is, in my view, a transformation. It is not simply the industrial era, 'amped up on tech steroids'. The digital era is much more than just a continuum of the industrial era (as suggested by the Davos-sponsored term: Industry 4.0). It is an economic and possibly even an anthropological transformation, which requires nothing less than an overhaul of current industrial era business models.

This requires much more than fronting your business model with a mobile app, or sponsoring a hackathon. It requires a 'drains up' reengineering of the business. But, of course, such a transformation would be guaranteed to destroy your existing cash flows, without any guarantee of creating new ones. Thus, we must factor this into the journey to be taken.

Nonetheless, for most industrial era organisations nothing less than a transformation is required. Again, an industrial era business, as defined in the previous chapter, is less defined by what it sells and its channels to market, and more about its approach to innovation, leadership and uncertainty.

Digital?

Hopefully by now you are recognising that digital is not simply:

- The opposite of analogue.
- A synonym for IT.

I am going to share my own perspectives on this a little later in the book. But for now, let's see what management consulting firm, McKinsey and Co. have to say on this.

In broad terms, they accept that technology has a role to play, that it embraces new ways of engaging with customers, and might even represent an entirely new way of doing business.

In more focused language, they talk about unlocking value at new frontiers through greater market sensitivity through the use of sensor-captured data. They talk about understanding the customer journey and experience, and fostering loyalty through contextualising the experience in the light of the journey. Using automation to both drive down costs, and to simplify the customer experience is part of becoming a digital business. All true as far as I am concerned, but it still hasn't got to the core of what digital is. Nonetheless, this definition helps us understand that there is a lot to be done in respect of our business models.

For now, I hope you are developing a sense as to why the industrial era business model is no longer fit for purpose. As mentioned, I will reveal my own perspectives on this at the appropriate point in the book. I suspect you already have a sense as to where I am heading.

What is the Biz 4.0 blueprint?

The Biz 4.0 blueprint identifies the key elements we need to consider when building a business fit for the digital era. At the very least, it can serve as a check list/self-assessment tool in respect of your organisation's 'digital age readiness'. I have developed it to help business leaders through the transformation process. But the principles go back millions of years, and are thus tried and tested.

There are three underlying assumptions to this model. You may not necessarily agree with all three. But if you bear with me, I will make the case for each of these in the course of this book. The assumptions being:

1. Businesses exist to create value for their stakeholders, of which shareholders are a subset.

2. If we consider the business as a tribe, and develop a tribal mindset, we will be in a better position to thrive in the digital age.

3. Humans have certain anthropological drivers that, if met, will increase their engagement with the business.

The strategic approaches developed for the industrial era are no longer fit for purpose, hence the development of the Biz 4.0 blueprint.

Let's look at each assumption in turn:

Capital: The Five value generators

1. *Businesses exist to create value for their stakeholders, of which shareholders are a subset.*

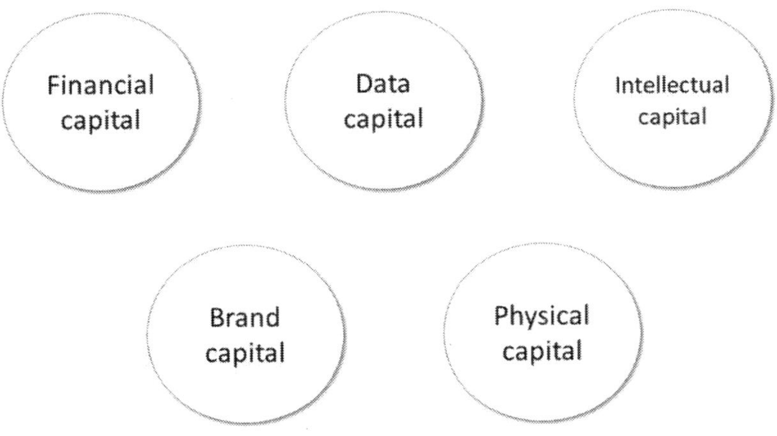

Figure 2 The five value generators

This should be the least controversial of the assumptions. Businesses need to create value, so that, at the very least, would-be customers do not decide that they are better off creating the products or services themselves. Shareholders are expecting that their investment yields a better return than that emerging from leaving their cash on deposit. In fact, they are looking for a significantly greater return, given the greater risk they are incurring.

So clearly capital can take the form of money, or assets that can quickly, or eventually, be converted into money, for example, government bonds or land. Such assets, which include cash, are called **financial capital**. Financial capital is explicitly documented on an organisation's balance sheet. It is often used as a term to refer to the cash acquired to grow the business, for example through the issuance of bonds and shares. I will use this term in respect of the organisation's cash or cash equivalents stockpile. The primary motive for businesses is to grow this stockpile. With a larger stockpile, you can acquire more companies, please shareholders and/or genuinely help society.

A quick definition on assets. These are the items that contribute to the creation of capital. Assets tend to grow in value, or are at least expected to grow in value.

Then there is what is called **physical capital**. Traditionally this would include the physical items used to enable production, such as buildings, raw materials, machinery and land. NB. We also mentioned land under financial capital. In that case, it is purely held as an investment, and not as a necessary element of the running of the business. Physical capital is also represented on the balance sheet.

Brand capital, better known as brand equity, is an important source of value. It enables businesses to charge more because of the brand association the customer enjoys in respect of, say, owning a Louis Vuitton handbag. At the luxury end of the market, brand capital is taken to the extreme, where the price has nothing to do with the item's cost of production, and has all to do with the fact that it is priced beyond the reach of most consumers. Brand capital was not generally expressed on the balance sheet, though today it can be found embedded in the intangible assets section.

Intellectual capital reflects how humans have value beyond being a mindless cog in the machine. Your people have the capacity to create things, the template of which has saleable value. The relationships your people build with the market are also a source of intellectual capital. Again, this is bundled in with intangible assets on the balance sheet. As we move to a more service-oriented world, organisations will need to find ways of expressing intellectual capital in a more explicit manner.

The new kid on the block is **data capital**. We have been storing data electronically now for several decades. In recent years, the market has become excited about 'big data'. As business models gravitate from boardroom gut-feelings to data-driven decision making, the value of the organisation's data repositories will become more significant. Again, today many organisations are either, as mentioned, 'burning the gas', or collecting it, but with no idea of how to monetise it. This is, in my experience, hardly acknowledged by anyone as a source of value creation in economic terms. I implore economists to create a model whereby this can be explicitly expressed on the organisation's balance sheet.

So, there you have it, the five main sources of capital. We will drill down on these in a subsequent chapter. My aim at this stage is simply to make some gentle introductions. Not all economists will agree on my apportioning of the elements that make up the organisation's capital portfolio. Computers might be considered a physical asset, or a key element of intellectual capital. The point here is not so much to pinpoint where the elements are apportioned, but that we are aware of the main sources of value creation in business.

Business leaders who intend to position their organisations for longevity need to monitor progress in these five areas, because the whole point of a business is to create value. Smart business leaders will build assets which themselves not only represent value, but create it too.

Success factors: The Five As

2. *If we consider the business as a tribe, and develop a tribal mindset, we will be in a better position to thrive in the digital age.*

These success factors have been inferred from my observations in respect of tribal behaviour. More specifically, my observations on the observations of tribal behaviour by genuine anthropologists. My reasoning being that we have spent most our time on the planet as hunter gatherers.

It is generally considered that significant adaptations in humans takes about 25,000 years. Circa 12,000 years ago, we were all hunter gatherers. Despite the radical differences, we can note when comparing the world of the hunter gatherer to modern society, we are personally still wired to be tribal hunter gatherers. So, we might as well rekindle a tried and tested (over many millennia) winning formula in favour of the factory models we have endured for only a few centuries.

It is important not to deny the economic boost the industrial era delivered. But it is a model that has left nearly everyone, excluding the 'factory owners', miserable in the process.

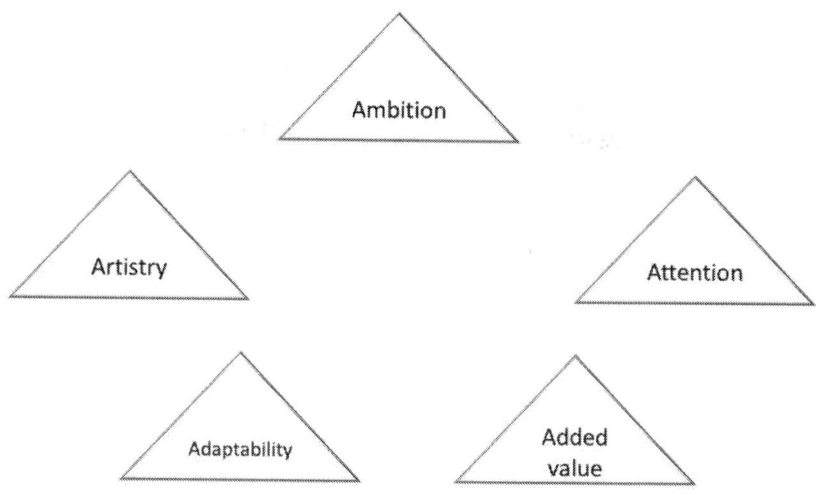

Figure 3 The five success factors

Whilst there are many success factors I could focus on, including thumbs, brachiation (the ability to move our arms in almost any direction, which was very useful when we lived in the trees, and underpins advances in tennis) and an optimised brain to weight ratio, I have chosen, perhaps self-servingly, to choose characteristics that map more readily onto the world of business. Looking at these in turn:

The tribe had a collective **ambition**. Most likely it didn't extend much beyond surviving long enough to create the next generation. This ambition required a *strategy* of sorts. It also required the capacity to *innovate*, along with a cohesive *culture* that shared the ambition.

The tribe had to pay **attention** at all times. The snapping of a twig, or an escalating argument between two members could signal trouble. The former could be indicative of a stealthy invading tribe; the latter could be indicative of a tribal schism. The *cognitive capacity* of the tribe was valued. Tired and inattentive members could put the tribe or themselves at risk. The use of *sensors* in the form of reconnaissance teams and sentry guards added to the tribe's capacity to monitor what was happening in its environment, and thus optimise the manner in which it engaged with the environment. The arrival of an attacking tribe, or the detection of potential prey required strong situational analysis, and thus smart *decision making*, a life-preserving skill on the unforgiving savanna.

The tribe could not afford to carry passengers. Everyone contributed in some way, whether that be as a hunter, gatherer or warrior. Often people were expected to switch roles based on the situation. Nonetheless the roles necessary to keep a tribe functioning required specific skills and capabilities.

Whilst being good at your role would not lead to sponsorship deals, or a corner office, it would come with enhanced social status. Thus, the tribe valued **artistry**, the ability to perform skilfully at the highest level. Like any artist, they had a deep desire to improve their *performance*, they weren't in it for the resources perks. In any case, anything less than equitable sharing was frowned upon.

Fear of being drummed out of the tribe, which was the equivalent of a death sentence, ensured that the tribal members were *motivated* to perform at the top of their game. Importantly, it wasn't enough to do a good job, but to be known for doing good work. So, they needed to ensure their fellow tribesmen were aware of their contribution. Thus, the concept of *personal branding* was key to tribal membership. Many tribes today will treat greed and cowardice as traits that only execution can remedy. So, ensuring you were perceived as a solid team player was nothing less than a survival skill.

Tribes were not hermetically-sealed from reality. They didn't live in centrally-heated accommodation, and they didn't have ready access to a 24-hour store, replete with season-agnostic ready-meals. Tribes ate what they killed/picked. **Adaptability** was an important tribal characteristic. Not only did they need to adapt to their *macroeconomic* circumstances, which in those days more or less boiled down to terrain, predators, food sources and weather, they needed to establish whether nearby tribes represented *competition*, or a potential *market* with whom they could trade.

Not all tribes traded. Some took a 'just in time' approach to existence, and so consumed everything they caught. But some would build a surplus of goods, which could be traded. Tribes continuously adapted to the market. With the arrival of the pastoralists, they took the opportunity to forge trading links. Even today, tribes trade with industrial communities.

To trade, tribes would need to be able to **add-value** in the eyes of the target market. In other words, they would need to provide offerings at a price that caused the potential buyer to trade, rather than go elsewhere, or do it themselves. These offerings may have been *human-based*, for example, selling slaves, or offering mercenary services to peace-loving tribes that needed a problem resolved. Or the offerings may have been *technology-based,* in that the buyer would receive tangible goods such as food, spears or pelts that required some degree of manufacturing. In respect of developing an offerings catalogue, so to speak, the tribe had to have some sort of *methodology* to establish:

- What the market required.
- What it would stomach price-wise.
- How to develop and evolve the offering in the light of changing demand.

For the purposes of recollection, these five success factors all conveniently start with the letter 'A'. As we will see, they are also key areas of focus for businesses in the digital age.

Human drivers: The 9 essentials

3. *Humans have certain anthropological drivers that if met will increase their engagement with the business.*

Humans found a role in the industrial era by virtue of the limitations of technology. Technology consistently delivered, didn't get hangovers, or have management-draining career aspirations. However, at the outset of the industrial era, there was much that technology was unable to do.

This proved to be an economic opportunity for humans, so many people raced from the villages to the city to get a piece of the economic action by literally becoming a piece of the economic machine.

But the price of being paid was to generally do work we didn't enjoy, whilst suppressing all our natural tendencies. Once we had learnt how to be an effective technology placeholder, we were expected to behave like a piece of technology during the working day.

Productivity
Curiosity
Courage
Spirituality

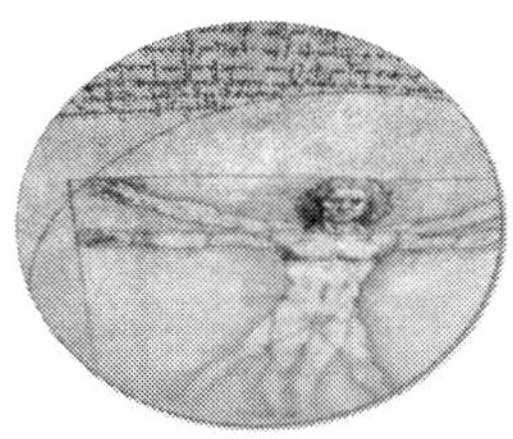

Mobility
Sociality
Work-life integration
Creativity
Decision making

Figure 4 The 9 anthropological drivers

Specifically, the natural tendencies/anthropological drivers we had to suppress included the desire to:

- Be mobile.
- Be social.
- Have a life where work and our personal life were more integrated.
- Be creative.
- Make our own decisions.
- Be curious.
- Be productive.
- Be courageous.
- Be spiritual.

We will explore these in more detail shortly, and provide some justification for their inclusion. Smart organisations such as Facebook and Google get this, and have built their organisations accordingly. In the context of what you have read so far, you might reflect on why organisations bother with pot plants and tropical fish tanks? And why some include fireman's poles, and give their teams autonomy over the way in which their office is designed. We are coming to the end of the road in respect of humans as cog workers/technology placeholders in the industrial machine. The technology is fast approaching the ability to more or less do everything the 'factory' requires.

The value from humans is increasingly originating from what we can do that technology has yet to master. The good news for us is that it plays to our innate capabilities, which we have nurtured over many millennia. The world's most powerful computers can learn very quickly thanks to artificial intelligence, but our intelligence has had millions of years of programming, and debugging, so we still have a lot to offer.

Digital age workers will feel more human and alive than their predecessors. But they will need to operate at the peak of their human capability. Those with a high-performance athlete's mindset will relish this new world. Those hoping to sail below the radar into a lush retirement will be sorely disappointed.

So, in terms of the Biz 4.0 template, think 5-5-9. Five sources of value, five success factors and nine anthropological drivers.

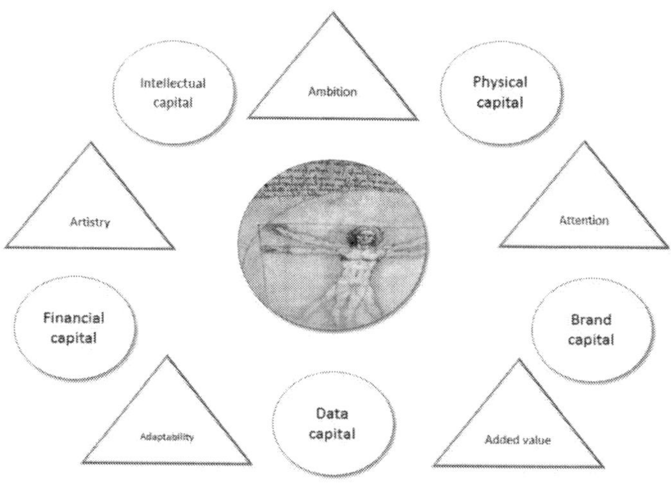

Figure 5 The Biz 4.0 blueprint

Next up, we will look at the three main elements of Biz 4.0 in a little more detail.

Take note

- Keep in mind that the primary focus of a business is to create value. So, there must always be a correlation between the organisation's activities and the five value generators.

- Now that technology is starting to obviate the need for humans, the only way to keep humans in play is to ensure they deliver value over and above the capabilities of new technology.

- The point is not to find a way to keep humans in work, despite the rise of the robots, but to harness our natural instincts to create even more value than the technology can generate. From an anthropological perspective, there is no dignity in industrial era labour.

- The issue of keeping humans busy/off the streets should not be a concern for business owners. Paternalism, leads to worker infantilism, which has a denaturing effect. Protecting the workers, despite the market realities, is just denying them the opportunity to develop their digital savanna survival skills.

3 The five value creators

Overview

In this chapter, we look at the five main value creators introduced earlier as part of the Biz 4.0 blueprint. We will explore the importance of value creation, along with how it is created.

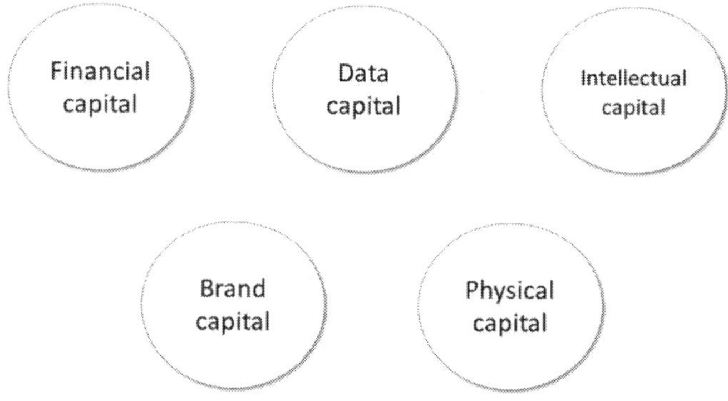

Figure 6 The five value generators

This is important because...

If your business is not in the business of creating value, it is unlikely that you will be in business for very long.

Value, capital and assets

Let's be clear on these interrelated terms. Value can be considered as a representation of the benefit of owning something. Owning a phone provides me with functional value in that I can work whilst on the move, and thus make better use of time and be more responsive.

Perhaps owning the phone confers a certain status. It might suggest that I am of a certain socio-economic class, and most likely to be creative. So, it has brand value. And if I was ever in financial difficulties, I could easily sell it, so it has financial value. The phone, or any other source of value, is known as an asset. Though as we will see shortly, not all assets are the same in respect of their perpetual value generating capabilities. From a business perspective, assets are purchased or created to generate cash flow, reduce expenses and/or improve sales.

Capital might be thought of as the financial value of an asset. Money is the purest form of capital. It can be used immediately for the purposes of making a purchase. Shares are also a form of capital. My ability to readily convert shares into cash will depend on the extent to which there is market liquidity. An asset such as a nuclear reactor will require a significant lead time if the intention is to convert it into cash.

Perhaps confusingly, capital is a term used to refer to cash and other financial assets, but also used to refer to any asset, which has a financial value. So, the term asset and capital are interchangeable in the context of financial value.

Assets are often classified as current or fixed. Current assets are defined as those that can be converted into cash within one year. Outstanding invoices due, but not yet paid, would from an accounting perspective be considered current assets. Fixed assets are not so easily turned into cash, for example, factory equipment. From an accounting perspective, such assets are considered to depreciate over time, and so this must be factored into the balance sheet. But there are assets, and there are assets. And this is a critical distinction for digital age businesses. Let's look at the three main types of assets:

Depreciating assets

Anything that drops in value over time is a depreciating asset. Whilst one can squeeze value from the asset, that value will decrease over time. And even if it doesn't decrease in this respect, it will eventually break, or the market will be increasingly less inclined to pay the original price if it had to be exchanged for cash.

Cars are a good example of a depreciating asset. Depreciating assets are not considered good long-term financial investments. Many would argue that such assets are better rented in the form of a service than bought outright. Computing hardware, and even software, fall into this category. This digital era reality is steadily dawning on the business world. You will be familiar with 'the cloud'. If not, then I would make this a priority.

The realisation that buying a car is not the smartest use of one's capital is forcing the automotive industry to reconsider its value proposition. And no doubt this realisation is a boon to the likes of Uber and Zipcar. Business models in many respects mimic nature. One organism's misfortune provides fertile conditions for another. Fungus on decaying food comes to mind.

Dormant assets

Dormant assets typically do not decrease in value, particularly over the longer term. However, once they are acquired, their financial value is locked into the asset until it is sold. A block of gold would be an example. Thus, dormant assets tie up your capital. But you are willing to make this near-term sacrifice for the prospect of long-term benefit.

You may still gain some value by virtue of owning a dormant asset such as your home (shelter), or a rare piece of artwork (enjoyment). But you would have to sell them to realise their financial value (though as we will shall see shortly, even these dormant assets can be activated). And given the uncertainty and volatility in the market, there is no guarantee that what started out as a dormant asset will even be an asset at the time of sale.

This is akin to investing in growth stocks. The companies concerned have great potential, but they are not at a stage where they can consistently make a profit, and so do not pay dividends. Thus, they represent a dormant asset. However, if all goes well, they will morph into an active asset.

Active assets

Active assets not only generally increase in value, but they generate an income because of their ownership. If you were to rent out a room in your property that dormant asset would become active. Similarly, if you were to charge people to look at your rare piece of artwork. The shares of companies that pay an annual dividend to shareholders would be considered an active asset.

In effect, your capital investment is generating wealth for you in both the short and long term. In some respects, this is mitigating the risk of investing in things that through unforeseen circumstances cease to be assets.

It is my view that businesses should be in the business of investing in and creating active assets. Thanks to the laws of compound interest, active assets are much more valuable than their net increase in value plus the sum of all dividend payments/room rentals/admissions. As these regular payments come in, they can be invested in further active assets, giving rise to an exponential degree of growth. This is shareholder-pleasing. It is also customer-pleasing because more capital generally equates to greater investment in products and services.

The problem with value creation

Corporations are expected to make a profit, so that shareholders can enjoy a dividend payment, usually annually, on their investment. But investors are expecting that overall value of the company to grow as well, so that when it comes to selling their shares, they will be worth more than the purchase price. Business leaders, ie. those tasked with making the shareholders smile, have thus to strike a balance between profit generation and value creation. A focus on the former leads to short term thinking, and an aversion to risk. Value creation traditionally required taking a longer view. If business leaders take a longer-term view, they are running the risk of making themselves look bad, and their successors look good. Investment costs money, and so will negatively impact profits in the short term, with no guarantee of boosting profits in the long term.

Whilst there are some very long-serving CEOs, the typical life expectancy for a Fortune 500 CEO is under five years. So, if they want to make a positive and high profile impression, they will likely focus on profits, at the expense of value creation.

Of course, there are sectors where there is no choice but to play a long game; automotive and pharmaceuticals come to mind. Similarly, there are organisations which have over time built up impressive cash-generating brands, and are not likely to trade them in for a quick profit, unless extreme circumstances dictate such a move.

Capital focus

I have already made the case for investing in/creating active assets. Short-termism causes many business leaders to ignore this and just focus on the near-term bottom line. Poor articulation of what constitutes an asset, coupled with what it is actually worth, makes capital management a hazy science. If the Chief Finance Officer (CFO), or the shareholders, cannot see an obvious correlation between the CEO's asset building activities and the financial health of the organisation, then such initiatives will be frowned upon.

Some investments are obvious, such as buying a patent to complement the existing portfolio of cancer drugs. But investing millions on a new, slightly elongated version of the existing corporate logo is less so. Life was simpler at the outset of the industrial era. The primary value in goods was in their functional capabilities. Originally, industrial era organisations were valued purely based on their financial and physical assets. The difference between the market value, ie. what the market was willing to pay for the organisation, and the sum of the physical and financial assets would be attributed to some sort of 'dark' value creation that magically came about by the alchemy of mixing money with buildings, people and equipment.

Over time this intangible value was represented on the corporate balance sheet as 'intangible assets'. Today, beyond the baseline expectation of product/service utility, these intangible assets are expected to provide consumers with:

- A lifestyle marker.
- Access to other similar consumers.
- Real-time analytics to optimise the use of the product or service in question.

So clearly the assets of the organisation today need to extend beyond money and property (eg. buildings, machinery, vehicles, raw materials). As we will see, these new assets are very good news for all stakeholders.

A question arises as to how we account for the workers. In the industrial era, they provided horsepower, so in that sense they were raw materials. They were also technology placeholders, so in that respect they were machinery (or at least a component). Either perspective is of course incorrect from both an accounting and moral perspective. The organisation doesn't own the workers, in the sense of slavery, though there may well be economic slavery in play, particularly when it is a buyer's market from a labour perspective.

From an accounting perspective, there is the issue of the assets leaving the factory each evening, and no-one knowing for sure whether they will return the next day. Imagine each evening, putting your valuables out on the street, with an expectation they will be there in the morning. This is possibly why the laudable notion of human capital has not really gained traction. Humans are a somewhat risky component of business. That is why the factory owners reduced their role to swappable machinery components. This is the basis of job specifications, and as we will see, why they increasingly no longer serve a useful purpose. Let us now revisit the five sources of value, which were detailed in the Biz 4.0 blueprint chapter.

Financial capital

Financial capital is essentially cash generated by the business, or cash acquired by the business for the purposes of running, growing, changing, or saving the business.

Acquiring cash from outside the business can take the form of a loan or the surrendering of equity. The former is often referred to as a bond, the latter as a share.

Businesses need to make a cash surplus to be of interest to shareholders. Sometimes this surplus cash is redistributed to shareholders in the form of dividend payments. Sometimes it is invested in assets that will enhance the organisation's effectiveness, for example, to buy new machinery. Sometimes it may be used in part, or in full, to acquire other organisations.

Businesses do not want to start each financial year with zero cash, so they will retain a surplus to:

- Ensure there is enough working capital for the smooth operation of the business.
- Provide a buffer/war chest, just in case a threat emerges or there is a drop off in sales.
- Capitalise on unexpected opportunities, such as the purchasing of an ailing rival.

This cash could be retained in a corporate bank account, as this would generally make for easier access. However, the cash would be generating negligible interest, and thus might even be devaluing as inflation grows at a rate higher than the associated account interest rate.

This takes us into the arena of treasury management. It is the CFO, or treasury manager's function to sweat the cash as much as possible, whilst keeping in mind the attendant risks of investing, and ease of access.

Thus, the treasury manager might use the cash to:

- Buy shares in other companies.
- Buy back the company's own shares.
- Buy foreign currencies.

- Build an investment portfolio of land and property that it then rents out.
- Acquire art.
    - Invest in financial instruments that serve to protect the organisation against failure in its main investments. Insurance policies come to mind, as well as derivative instruments.
    - Derivatives themselves can be used to gain significant returns on one's cash. Though this is more speculation than investment. And sometimes the losses can exceed the initial sum invested.

I recognise that the typical reader of this book does not need a primer on financial management. However, it will help to keep this in mind when we soon look at an emerging asset class, to which very few senior executives are giving consideration.

Physical capital

At the outset of the industrial era it would have been difficult to conduct business without a factory, vehicles, machinery, utilities, and raw materials, and of course people.

Physical capital can be defined as those assets that are necessary for the running of the business. From an accounting perspective, they represent assets that are not consumed in the process of conducting business. So strictly speaking raw materials are not physical capital; they are sometimes referred to as circulating capital. But the bottom line is that if the company goes into liquidation, these raw materials will likely generate cash through their disposal. So, for the purposes of this book, they can be thought of as physical assets.

The range of utilities we require in business today has evolved from the days when the primary energy supply was water flow. Back then, one might have bought a stretch of the river to ensure its availability, in as much as nature allowed. The arrival of steam and electricity would have required organisations to have their own energy production facilities.

But today, utilities are increasingly supplied by third parties who have the scale to provide it at a favourable rate when compared to managing energy production in-house.

In recent years, organisations are reassessing their perspectives on physical assets. Famed investor Warren Buffet has helped progress this thinking through his philosophy, which broadly states that if something appreciates in value then buy it, if not, then rent it'.

So rather than owning fleets of lorries and cars, many organisations use the services of fleet management/logistics companies. Whilst owning the factory/head office is a long-term investment, its maintenance is an ongoing cost, requiring specialised staff. If property management is not a competency of the organisation, it might make sense to outsource it to an organisation that offers 'property as a service'.

As the market becomes increasingly unpredictable, the ability to 'up sticks' and move the business to another location is important. So, whilst property might well be a solid financial investment, it is not necessarily the case when it comes to your place(s) of work.

This can equally apply to the machinery used by the organisation, including the computing infrastructure. Physical capital traditionally would have been a significant asset class. Today, it is possible for there to be no physical assets involved, with all physical requirements provided as a service. As a rule, the aim is to grow organisational value through capital growth. Physical capital is the exception. In the digital age, market nimbleness means being able to rapidly jump from say boot production to smartphones. And to expect such transitions on an increasingly regular basis.

The problem with physical capital in the ownership sense is that it locks you into an operating model that may ultimately serve the same purpose as concrete boots (think of the enemy disposal technique used by gangsters).

Therefore, unlike the other sources of capital, you are encouraged to reduce your exposure to physical capital. I have included it in this section for completeness, and to warn against the aforementioned risks.

Many organisations have taken this to its natural conclusion, and outsourced the manufacturing of its goods. The brand name on your computer or console is not necessarily a reference to the company that built the device. Thus, the key competencies of such companies distil down to branding and information management. Coincidentally, these are in fact key competencies of digital age organisations.

Brand capital

Brand capital, better known as brand equity, is an increasingly important concept. When I was young, one's choice of bank was largely based on the bank your parents used. Today, for many people, their choice of bank can be as much a reflection of the type of person they are, as the services provided. Perhaps for some:

- The association with 'old money' trumps slow service.
- The edgy social app interface trumps drug cartel money launderer.

In any case, the perception of an organisation is as important, if not more important than the truth about the organisation. As the saying goes, 'once you develop a reputation for getting up early, you can sleep until lunchtime'. Brand is like reputation, but as we will see shortly they are not quite the same.

Brand capital is a measurement of trust. That trust can be bestowed on specific offerings, or the organisation as a whole. Once a brand is established, it is critically important to protect it. Brand capital delivers value to the organisation because it makes the purchasing decision-making process easier for the consumer. If X makes it, then it must be a quality/good value product. Thus, the consumer is less price sensitive.

At the luxury end of the market, branding is everything. Luxury goods are expensive, not because they cost more to make, but because their unaffordability serves to send out a strong social signal from those who can afford to pay the premium.

Brand capital, despite it being such a tangible intangible (you can single out elements of the brand including, the logo, unique shaped bottle, intuitive user interface), has yet to consistently show up on the corporate balance sheet, beyond being bundled into the intangible assets section. Assigning a value that everyone agrees to is the challenge. It is fair to say that the closer one gets to the luxury/premium end of the market, the more intangible assets tend towards representing brand capital. But as we will see brand capital is not the only significant intangible.

Again, developing a brand means developing trust with the market. Developing trust means doing what you say, and delivering what you promise. Even at the retail end if the market, where margins are tight, selling washing powder that does not shred your underwear gives your product a significant advantage over a product that does.

Brands are important from a worker's perspective. There was a time when workers would simply ignore the purpose of their employer's business. Their personal economic needs outweighed the destructive nature of the company's offerings, whether they be landmines, cigarettes or confectionary. Of course, the employees may not have a choice of employers if they live in a small town and such a company is the only source of employment.

But today, people are much more conscious of the brand association they will inherit through their association with their employer's raison d'etre. The top brands recognise the importance of this association, and know that they can acquire great people, at favourable rates, because the brand association more than compensates for the salary shortfall.

In broader terms, brand capital might be better stated as brand equity plus reputation. Brand is a concern for the consumers. Reputation is a concern for everyone. Reputation covers the extent to which a corporation behaves like an upstanding citizen, having the interests of society at heart, and not just its pursuit of profits.

Employees, consumers and investors are increasingly drawn to organisations that take their social responsibilities seriously. So, reputation enhances the organisation's brand capital.

But we must retain some perspective on this. High-profile mistreatment of staff may have no impact on the brand, if the consumers cannot resist low cost offerings. Conversely, a solid brand may suffer at the hands of a damaged reputation. The BP Deepwater Horizon spill comes to mind. The quality of the gas did not change, but consumer preferences did. So sometimes brand will override shortfalls in reputation, and sometimes it won't. It is also unlikely that a great reputation will prop up a weak or damaged brand.

As a rule of thumb, particularly in this hyper-connected world, organisations should not cut corners when it comes to brand capital. Good news travels fast, but bad news travels faster. Small gains in brand capital can lead to significant changes in the organisation's fortunes.

The reverse, of course, is also true. Increasingly social media acts as an accelerant in this respect. In the digital age, the gap between market darling and social pariah is increasingly narrow. This makes investors nervous, so managing brand capital needs to be a priority.

Intellectual capital

Intellectual capital, like brand capital, is not a new concept, yet like brand capital, it is not usually explicitly detailed on the company's balance sheet, even though it can represent up to seventy percent of a company's value. It is likely that its association with innovation, and thus risk and cost, has led to this boardroom value-blindness.

Let us examine the three key elements of intellectual capital, namely:

- Human capital.
- Relational capital.
- Structural capital.

Looking at these, in turn:

Human capital

Traditionally this would have comprised the sum of the knowledge, experience, skills, qualifications, and competencies of the workforce. Low employee churn would have a positive impact on human capital. Humans in industrial era organisations, to this very day, have been largely compelled to follow the operations manual in respect of the business processes related to their role. Flair and creativity are generally frowned upon because they threaten the standardised nature of the factory/office processes and outputs.

As mentioned, such workers are going the way of the spinning jenny. Rote work lends itself to automation, and whether we like it or not, the robots are coming. What we are starting to see is the demand for people who do not slavishly follow the procedures, but through their creativity and other attributes create remarkable differentiated customer experiences that command a high margin.

There has always been an expectation that 'in the field'/'front of house' staff would have a high degree of emotional intelligence. The ability to empathise with the customer is important to resolving situations/concluding transactions to everyone's satisfaction. The trend I am witnessing is the need for all staff to have high emotional intelligence. Turning knowledge into wisdom, and more importantly into customer - pleasing action, requires collaboration between the workers.

It's okay to have an army of divas, so long as they suppress those idiosyncrasies that are likely to obstruct the collaborative process. Watch any primetime TV chat show, and you will notice that it is only those celebrities that play nicely with the others that tend to be invited back on the show.

Collaboration is the process where the exponential effects of human capital investment are manifested. In the digital age, more than ever, it is fair to say that it is not just what you know, but who you know. The social networks of your staff have corporate value. They in effect extend the company's brain trust, or at least bolster the crowdsourcing pool that the organisation can draw upon. That pool is a source of organisational value.

Perhaps the most interesting development in respect of human capital is the value to be found in the worker's experience. Not the corporate experience they have acquired throughout their working lives, but the experience that sits outside of their professional life. It could be that a worker's hobbies and interests can be applied to a challenge or opportunity the organisation is facing.

But then there are the experiences that one would perhaps never find detailed on a LinkedIn profile, because they are not considered 'professional'. These might include a period of mental illness, time spent leading a street gang, or a summer job that involved using pressure selling techniques to bully holiday makers into investing in timeshare apartments of questionable quality. Or in fact any experience that shows you are a human being with vulnerabilities and weaknesses.

It is not obvious how such experiences would fit into the traditional strategy of a modern-day corporation. But these experiences could well be the catalysts to create new strategies, for example:

Former mental health sufferer – Such experience could be used to open niche markets offering services and products optimised for those suffering mental ill health.

Gang leader – The organisation has been considering the possibility of opening a new office in a war-torn part of the planet. It is likely that the war will end in the foreseeable future, and being in at the start will give the organisation a first mover advantage. But to do this, the company needs someone who is both street wise and able to 'handle themselves'.

Pressure salesman – The procurement department is ill-equipped to deal with the psychological techniques used by increasingly desperate suppliers. A briefing from someone expert in those techniques, coupled with some countermeasures, would have a significant bearing on the organisation's cost structure.

Failing to tap the full potential of your people short-changes the customers, the company and the individual.

Now that we are starting to harness the capability of people in a more holistic way, we need to manage our talent in a manner not dissimilar to how parents care for their children. Losing an employee to a competitor is no longer akin to the loss of a consignment of stationery. It's not simply a case of phoning procurement to find a replacement, as it was in the industrial era. Modern workers are unique, and it is the sum of their uniqueness that makes the corporation unique.

Over time, I believe we will see a transition from the job specification, as an initiator of the hiring process, to a more talent-initiated approach. Strategy will be turned on its head, as talent management moves from being triggered by the strategy to triggering the strategy. There is an opportunity here for recruitment agencies that are prepared to raise their game above the buzzword bingo approach of matching job specifications to resumes. The HR function would be wise to review its capabilities in the light of this.

Relational capital

This represents the value generated by your relationships with key stakeholders in your ecosystem/extended tribe. Relational capital might include the degree of cordiality that exist between your organisation and:

- The media.
- Investors.
- Analysts.
- Customers.
- Suppliers.
- Government officials.

Classifying relationships on a spectrum covering hostile, transactional, advisory and personal can work well. By personal, I mean that communications extend beyond the professional domain into areas such as hobbies and family. You might say that this is veering towards friendship. On this spectrum one can overlay the transition from untrusted to trusted, and from irrelevant to relevant.

There is nothing new in trying to maintain good relationships with key people. But some organisations have been slow to wake up to the importance of developing genuine relationships with customers. The lifetime value of a customer far exceeds the gains made by a slick one-off hustle. And even amongst those that conceptually grasp customer relationship management, there are still those that see this as an exercise in controlling the customer, rather than a mutually supportive relationship. So, small talk quickly segues into the hustle.

There is much work to be done in this space. It often requires a significant reengineering of the associated sales management controls. This is never easy, but the upside of getting this right is very high. Happy customers talk to other customers. This network effect gives rise to exponential improvements in sales. Great relationships are forged by great people. When those people 'walk' so do their dividend-rich customer relationships. You can also wave goodbye to their social connections. Losing good business developers is careless intellectual capital management.

Structural capital

Structural capital can be considered as that aspect of intellectual capital that remains, even when people leave the organisation. It can be broken down into three sub-elements:

- Innovation capital.
- Process capital.
- Organisational capital.

Innovation capital – This covers the intellectual property that the organisation has acquired or created. Patents and trademarks come to mind. Whilst they do not always appear explicitly on the balance sheet, when it comes to selling them, they almost miraculously take on financial values. The associated figures are perhaps less associated with their objective value, and more a reflection of what the buyer might be willing to pay at that point in time. This is why balance sheet valuation is so difficult.

Process capital – This reflects the approach, methods and techniques by which the organisation does things. They become capital once they are institutionalised. That is to say, they are extracted from the heads of the relevant individuals and documented, so that the organisation is no longer reliant on those individuals for the smooth running of the organisation's processes.

An organisation that has a process model that is not dependent on a few experts, poses less of a risk to stakeholders, and in that respect, it can be seen as value-enhancing. Processes that can be provided as a service or franchised to other organisations will be of particular value.

Organisational capital – This is probably the most intangible of the intangibles, and therefore is the least likely to find its way onto the balance sheet in the near-term. The 'quality' of the following will have a bearing on organisational capital:

- Company vision.
- The culture.
- Structure.
- The learning and development function.
- IT systems.

In respect of IT systems, this is less a reference to the hardware or software packages owned or rented, but to the unique configuration/integration of the IT components, such that collectively they support the business in its creation of value.

As mentioned, in the latter stages of the industrial era, the notion of human capital emerged. Though the problem with humans is that they took flight every evening, with shareholders not knowing for sure, whether they would return the next day. But increasingly, as we have seen, these humans leave residues (intellectual property) that could be considered as assets of the organisation.

But the point is not to simply capture the human residue, but to provide the perfect conditions for people to do great work with other great people.

As a closing point on intellectual capital, I mentioned that raw materials were considered circulating capital. As organisations evolve in collaborative sophistication, I expect knowledge and wisdom to be considered a post-industrial variant of circulating capital. Just a thought.

Data capital

Data permeates every aspect of modern business. It is the raw material both acquired and produced by the organisation. Traditionally an organisation's data came from:

- Employee activity.
- Customer activity.
- Supplier activity.

These were simply accounting ledgers. But they moved beyond purely financial records as organisations started to collect data that would help:

- Squeeze more value from the staff.
- The business development staff get the next sale.
- Deepen the supplier relationship.

Today this data is complemented with data from:

- Professional data providers.
- Social feeds.
- Smart devices.

The deluge of data hitting the organisation on a daily basis has given rise to the term 'big data'. Some business leaders are so in the dark about big data that they ask their IT people to build or buy the company some big data, as if it is a product. Big data is an overused and hyped up term to flag the exponential growth in data because of real-time feeds (social and device) and video.

There is a genuine challenge in terms of linking the organisation's disparate data pools into one coherent model. It is only when this is achieved can your data truly form the basis of the organisation's decision making.

Failure to achieve this and your data becomes a corporate liability. But once achieved, you have created an asset that not only provides you with an accurate representation of your market, but also has the potential to identify new revenue streams.

All thing being equal, where two organisations have much the same data model, the one with the better analytics tools will gain the greatest benefit. If two oil exploration companies have access to the same oil field, the company with the best drilling equipment is most likely to strike oil, and maximise the extraction. And for every barrel they extract, it means one less barrel available for the poorly equipped company.

Keep in mind that this is not an arms race in respect of data volumes. The organisation with the 'biggest data' doesn't necessarily win. Choosing what to store and what to discard is an exercise not dissimilar to a humpback whale extracting plankton from the large volumes of water that passes through its mouth.

Therefore, organisations are encouraged to acquire people skilled in data architecture (data exploration), along with data scientists (data refiners) who will turn the data into information and insight. Insight that potentially could identify new markets, whilst they remain invisible to your competitors.

Insight generation will evolve from a source of competitive advantage to table stakes, as business models become increasingly data-driven. Gut feeling is making away for genuine data as the primary method for navigating the increasingly stormy marketplace.

Most organisations today are sitting on mounds of data with which they are doing very little. Possibly this isn't a bad thing, particularly if these mounds are currently not integrated into a coherent single-view model.

Imagine a board meeting where the CEO asks the question, "How have we sweated our data in the last month?". All eyes might initially turn to the CIO. But it is not her job to deliver value from the data asset, but to protect it, and provide tools to enable the users to extract the value. If I was the CEO, I would expect to hear statements from the other business leaders, such as:

- "We have identified our top 10 clients globally by revenue, and none of them are in our top 50 in Europe. We are thus reassigning our European account managers to address this gaping opportunity."
- "Thirty percent of our Twitter followers are in their twenties. Further analysis highlighted that stair lifts have become desirable accessories amongst tech sector hipsters. We plan to open a chain of pop-up stair lift stores located in areas undergoing rapid gentrification.

In the same way that the Finance department has a treasury management function, possibly there needs to be a data treasury management function, whose role is to maximise the return on the organisation's data. But it could also focus on creating new value streams by in effect creating new data. Imagine a furniture company that provides 'sitting analytics' (posture, duration), for a premium. This would simply require some sensors to be installed in the chairs.

As IoT, becomes more prevalent, there will be business leaders who remain unaware of the oil field they are sitting on. Or perhaps worse still, they are conscious of the oil field, but insist on burning the gaseous by-product (data), rather than selling it. Thus, they are underperforming in terms of value generation. Two important points must thus be kept in mind:

- Your organisation is likely to witness exponential growth rates in terms of data creation.
- There is money in data.

Whilst it often doesn't make sense to store all data that passes through your devices and IT systems, one must ask the question why Amazon stores everything, including all of its customers' keypresses.

Take note

- My depiction of the asset classes detailed in this chapter will not be universally agreed upon. Computer hardware might equally be placed under physical assets or intellectual capital. My primary point is to illustrate the main types of capital/value creators so that business leaders can factor them into their decision making. The details I have provided are purely for illustration purposes.

- Be in the business of acquiring/building assets that continuously create value, rather than those that lock in value until the point at which they are sold.

4 The five success factors

Overview

In this chapter, we will explore the five aforementioned success factors that served our ancestors so well to see whether they can be applied to the modern-day enterprise.

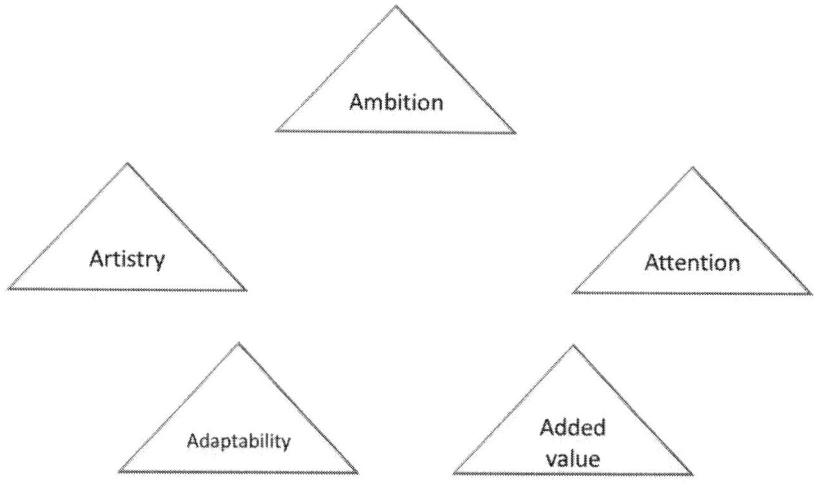

Figure 7 The five success factors

This is important because...

The assumptions upon which the industrial era rested are increasingly unsound. The industrial era model, which required people to do 'unnatural' work, relied on the economic power axis tilting towards the employer. Today the axis has swung the other way, in fact returning to its original position. So, we need to reengineer our enterprises accordingly.

Looking at each success factor (the five As) in turn:

Artistry

Back then

Artistry might at first seem to be a concept that has little relationship to either our ancestors or the modern enterprise. But if we consider artistry in the light of it being a measure of creative skill or ability, then it would certainly be a critical resource for the tribe.

There are many variables when it comes to hunting, gathering and warfare. And in respect of hunting and warfare, the other party often has a degree of guile that serves to make the associated processes even more challenging. Thus, requiring skilled tribe members.

The path to artistry was no doubt paved with failure and perhaps even coated with blood. Often the way to find out what worked was through discovering what didn't. Once the optimal skills were learnt, they would have been passed on to others in the tribe, and down through the generations.

Rather than fight, internal conflicts would sometimes lead to tribal splits, thus spawning a new tribe. Unless that tribe could acquire the survival-skills needed to operate in the hostile savanna, its prospects were bleak. So again, tribal members with specific creative skills were highly valued.

Today

Certain industries already recognise artistry in individuals. Thus, it is not simply a case of running a recruitment campaign to find a replacement Beyonce, because there is only one. The sports and entertainment world come to mind. In finance, there are star traders and fund managers. In automotive, there are sought-after car designers. Similarly, in architecture. So, the demand for artistry is already established at the top end of the employment pyramid.

In general, any competent car door fitter, knee surgeon or probate lawyer will do. In that sense, they are a commodity. Commodity work is prone to automation, not least because it is somewhat procedural in nature, and there is enough of it in demand to justify the investment in automation. The benefits of automating humans in the workplace have already been outlined. But these benefits are more focussed on cost, and error reduction, than on the unleashing of new value.

Humans still have a role to play in respect of creating new value. But it will involve only those humans who have not allowed the industrial era to denature their creativity. Such people can often appear somewhat maverick in nature. They often flout the rules, thus making their fellow cog workers uncomfortable; plus, they think for themselves. Being an artist/maverick is what will keep us out of the way of the digital age wrecking ball, particularly if we can integrate our human cognitive capabilities with the latest artificial cognitive technologies.

So, like our tribal ancestors, society and enterprise will come to increasingly value individual creativity. Or to put it another way, if you are not creative, you will be a burden on the tribe, and that doesn't generally end very well. This need for artistry, not just in one or two high profile people, but in all the workers, will change the dynamics of talent acquisition and retention. There is not enough of these people, and so the power axis is moving vigorously towards the worker. It will have repercussions on workplace design, and enterprise purpose, amongst other things.

Ambition

Back then

It is unlikely that our hunter gatherer ancestors had ambitions as we know them today in respect of dominating verticals, geographies or demographics. Beyond survival, the main goal was simply to enjoy being, which included the expression of our anthropological drivers, detailed earlier.

As we settled down to a life of agriculture, territory became more of an issue, particularly as population densities rose. Some clans would endeavour to pursue a largely peaceful existence. Others were more imperialistic in nature, possibly seeing the land of other tribes, or even the acquisition of their people, as a way of ensuring survival.

Some tribes would have latched onto the joys of trade, and thus created surpluses that could be used to obtain essential resources to which they would otherwise not have access.

Today

Today we have a similar spread in respect of enterprise ambition. Sometimes the market will set the tone. Hyper-competitive markets naturally lead to the need to acquire people with a competitive disposition.

Governments are supposed to govern in the interests of the citizens. Companies have traditionally focused on the owners. Voluntary organisations focus on those in need. So, as for our ancestors, different organisations/tribes/clans have different goals.

And even amongst these high-level classifications, organisational purpose can vary in subtle, and not so subtle ways. Today, in the developed world at least, we have talent fluidity, in the sense that people can choose to some extent which organisations they choose to work for. The remuneration may have a part to play in this, as might the social intentions of the organisation.

Thus, modern organisations need to choose their ambitions carefully, if they are to attract both the best 'buyers' and talent. With this in mind, they need to create an attractive culture to acquire and retain the best talent. And they need to innovate relentlessly to be attractive to the market. And all of this must be done within the context of a strategy that is fit for purpose in a volatile and uncertain world.

Attention

Back then

Paying attention was a survival skill. Hunter gatherers who trekked the savanna wearing MP3 players, or who were primarily focused on their social feeds were 'dead meat'. Similarly, tribes that were preoccupied with domestic matters were potentially leaving themselves exposed to hostile reality.

Stressed out tribes were less likely to make good decisions, and less likely to develop innovative ways to catch prey, leading to more stress.

Smart tribes learnt to read the signals in respect of the environment. They might notice indirect behaviours in, say, birds flying low, which might be indicative of rain. They might notice embers indicative that another tribe may be close by. Hunter gatherers who could pick up on signals, and particularly weak signals, could thus adapt their plans in respect of the data.

Today

Throughout the industrial era, the need to pay attention was seen as an event, as opposed to a discipline. If you wanted to tune in to what the market wanted, you might conduct some market research. There was such a degree of certainty that once you found your market niche, or even position of market dominance, you could sit back and count the coins. The world has of course changed. Success today is no indicator of success tomorrow. Your arch rival may not exist today, but may well have destroyed your business within a year.

Many organisations are replete with people, yet their brains lie untapped. Rather than harness the collective cognitive capacity of our people, we have them doing work so tedious that no doubt at some point even the robots will refuse to do.

"Here I am, brain the size of a planet and they ask me to take you down to the bridge. Call that job satisfaction? 'Cos I don't.",

Marvin the Paranoid Android, The Hitchhiker's Guide to the Galaxy.

Smart organisations are waking up to the power of their people. They are also waking up to how new technologies are enabling organisations to sense the market, and in turn make better decisions.

Added-value

Back then

Adding value became an important concept when tribes realised that they could gain value by trading surpluses they had acquired in respect of food. Pelts and pottery could also be found in the product catalogue.

Over ten thousand years ago, American Indians mined quartzite for the purposes of trading spearheads, knives and other scrapping tools. When the Romans arrived in the UK over two thousand years ago, they found evidence of international trading posts. So, the idea of trading is not new. In fact, some trading posts were seasonal, so the concept of a pop-up exchange/store is not new either.

Innovation was a key aspect of tribal innovation. Mimicking, or harnessing nature can be seen in the use of herbs for medicinal purposes, and bamboo for blowpipes. The extraction of dart poison from the latex of trees required a manufacturing process of circa one week duration.

The decision to launch a product or service likely came about as a result of there being an established demand, rather than as an arbitrary innovation backed up by an omni-channel/cross media marketing campaign. As well as increasingly sophisticated products, services were also traded. Examples include the trading of slaves and the provision of protection through 'mercenaries for hire'.

Today

Products and services continue to lie at the heart of trade today. The manufacturing processes may have become more sophisticated, but the idea of creating value that justifies payment beyond the cost of provision remains. Even the public sector today needs to think in terms of adding value. Increasing mobility means that citizens are evaluating where they can get the best 'life return' on their tax dollars, and are migrating accordingly. As the citizens (talent) migrate to high value societies, the employers will follow the citizens. Governments need to become acutely aware of their citizen value proposition, and nurture it, or risk becoming an economic backwater.

Today, what the market says, and what it does, are often two different things. Market research might tell you that your product is a winner, but when your target customers are asked to put their hands in their pocket, the reality is different. Thus, a more tentative live prototyping approach is taken today. The minimum viable product (MVP) model is the Silicon Valley approach to engaging with the market.

Humans today make a significant contribution to product and service provision. Though the numbers on the product-side have reduced dramatically with the automation of blue collar work. Netflix has harnessed new technologies such that there is no longer a need to hire film reel mounters, or ticket tearing specialists. We are in the early stages of watching the white-collar sequel.

Consulting today requires people to be involved. Software will increasingly provide the necessary support, possibly using case-based reasoning. For how much longer will Uber need drivers? Perhaps an indicator that your profession is coming up for extinction is when your boss is an algorithm.

Business in general had natural 'barriers to entry' at the outset of the industrial era. The capital outlay of building a factory being one such hurdle for a would-be challenger. Today any teenager, from their bedroom, can outsource every aspect of the business from manufacturing through to sales and marketing, to create a global empire. Unless your organisation is protected by regulation, the only way it can thrive is by relentless marketing-pleasing innovation.

Adaptability

Back then

The world was a perilous place. Hunter gatherers could not hermetically-seal themselves from the real world in a comfortable air-conditioned building, and conduct their lives virtually, like many of us do today. It was a gritty existence.

An abundance of berries this year was not an indication that that would be the case in subsequent years. Resilience was key to survival, and adaptability was key to resilience. Hunter gatherers had to morph from fruit pickers to predators as the needs of the tribe dictated.

As trade became an important part of tribal survivability, so then did the need to handle competition, and foster loyalty in the target market.

Today

The world turned more slowly in the early industrial era. Competition was easily recognisable, and if necessary could be overwhelmed by embarking on a price war knowing their financial reserves were less than yours. Political influence could also be applied. And as a last resort, there was always technology innovation, particularly in respect of operational efficiency.

Modern globalisation, fuelled by imperialism, opened new markets, and deepened economies of scale, thus, making it difficult for new entrants to get involved. In time, many markets reached an equilibrium comprising a handful of dominant players, with the rest occupying ecosystem niches.

Today, being a large organisation that enjoys market dominance is not a sure-fire indicator of future success. Competition is emerging in different guises from unlikely angles.

For example, the established car industry is not under threat from new manufacturers, such as Tesla, but from a societal trend away from car ownership. And witnessing the respect the established financial institutions are giving the fintech start-ups is akin to watching a nature documentary where a mouse is dictating territory terms to an elephant.

Increased connectivity, brought about new technologies, has led to greater volatility. A war in a distant land can have a bearing on the local price of goods. Natural disasters can have a disruptive impact on global supply chains. Currency wars and trade tariffs can drive a wedge between keen buyers and vendors.

Consumers are becoming increasingly shrewd. For example, they no longer believe that cigarettes are both urbane and healthy. And they don't like slick salespeople trained in 'getting us to yes'. Very few people today, on accepting a LinkedIn invitation, rejoice at the immediate pitch that follows their acceptance. We know selling is essential, but we don't like to be sold to in a seemingly untargeted and value-free manner.

With such uncertainty and volatility in the market, a key characteristic of a digital organisation is its ability to adapt to the realities of the market. The ability to abandon, or at least modify the strategic plan in the light of cold reality is important. Strategic planning is more akin to war than, say, building pyramids. With the latter, once you have the land, tools, materials and labour in place, you are good to go. With the former, as boxer Mike Tyson wisely pointed out, "everyone has a plan until they are punched in the mouth". The ability to recover quickly from a knock and keep moving forward, often in a dazed state, is the reality for business in the digital age.

Missing gaps

So, based on reviewing our existence over all time, artistry, ambition, attention, adding value and adaptability, as I have somewhat conveniently chosen to label them, are the key success factors for businesses in the digital age.

These success factors seem to contradict the traditional functional model of industrial era businesses. Which success factor represents Finance, and which one is HR? The traditional functional model is based on organisational convenience, rather than the convenience of the customer and the worker. Now that the power has shifted away from the factory owner, the model requires an overhaul.

But gaps appear to remain such as:

- Where is risk managed?
- Who handles governance?
- Where do we put the legal team?

Or perhaps they may generate some confusion:

- Is 'mergers and acquisitions' an ambition, adaptability or an adding value activity?
- Is information security an adaptability or an attention concern?

We will cover these and other concerns later in the book. We will also explore each success factor, and its key elements in more detail.

Take note

- The success of our tribal ancestors is key to organisational success in the digital age, particularly as the artificial structures of the industrial model cease to be fit for purpose.

- These five success factors cut across the traditional functional structure of industrial era organisations. To build a business where only the brains of a handful of people are utilised is outmoded and organisationally arthritic.

5 The nine anthropological drivers

Overview

In this chapter, we will cover the important traits that define us as human.

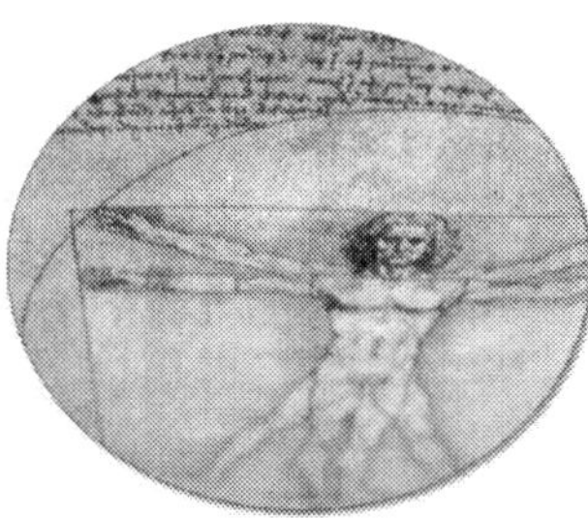

Figure 8 The 9 anthropological drivers

This is important because...

Once we understand what makes us human, we can build organisations that accommodate, and even capitalise on our natural inclinations.

A brief history of mankind

Hunter gatherer era

For the vast majority of our time on the planet, we have been hunter gatherers. As mentioned, we are still wired this way. As hunter gatherers:

- We were mobile. Our ancestors would cover many kilometres each day pursuing prey, and searching for new sources of berries.
- We were social. Coordinating the capturing of 'lunch', required the hunting group to collaborate. Poor collaboration might lead to being eaten by lunch.
- Our work and private lives were somewhat integrated. If the tribe hadn't eaten for a several days, then the appearance of food on the horizon at 18:01 wouldn't result in deferring its pursuit until 09:00 the next day.
- What with prey being intelligent, we had to be creative in how we secured our food.
- We had to make decisions, often in real-time, in respect of securing the food. Poor decisions could lead to no dinner that evening.
- We were judged on our productivity. No matter how hard we worked, or how long our working day, if we returned to the camp with no food, it was a bad day at the office.
- We were curious. Is the berry edible? What lies over the horizon? If it wasn't for this curiosity, we would still be spending most of our day roaming the savanna looking for food.
- We were courageous. Taking the next step, after our curiosity is piqued, required a degree of courage. Let's see whether I can get to the other side of the lake by sitting in this prototype canoe.

- We were spiritual, in that we contemplated the wider universe our role in it. Similarly, we contemplated the afterlife and our role in it. Ancient artifacts and megaliths attest to this.

Agricultural era

Around twelve thousand years ago, we settled by the oases, domesticated plants and animals, and became farmers.

As an agriculturalist:

- We continued to be mobile, though not as much as our ancestors.
- We were highly social. Developing a reputation as a trustworthy trader required good social skills.
- Work and life were integrated. Animals did not give birth on a 'nine to five' basis. This continues to be the case.
- There are many variables in farming, and so we had to be creative in terms of how we addressed the many unique challenges that emerged.
- We had to make decisions about both the present and the future.
- We were judged on our productivity. No crops, no buyers.
- We were curious. Our explorations into plant breeding and animal husbandry gave rise to increasingly hardy crops and animals.
- We were courageous. Again, experimenting with new techniques ran the risk of failure, which could mean death if no harvest ensued.
- We were spiritual. In ancient Egypt, the various agricultural activities, such as planting seeds and harvesting crops, took place at specific times in keeping with the plans of the gods. Animal sacrifices were a form of divine taxation.

Industrial era

Around two hundred years ago, we saw a fundamental change in the nature of work. The factory system came into being. Machines took over hand production methods. It heralded the era of entrepreneurism, and the standard of living for the general population started to increase steadily.

People raced from the villages to the towns to secure factory jobs, and in turn, economic prosperity. The very nature of daily life was changed, including:

- The end of mobility. Every day we turned up to the same building, and occupied the same space for the duration of the working day.
- The end of sociality. We were now paid for our time, as opposed to our output. So, talking on the factory line was discouraged.
- The end of work-life integration. Now, whilst at work, you were owned by the factory. Personal matters would have to wait until the end of the day. We generally didn't enjoy factory work, so we looked forward to the end of the day, the weekend, and the end of our working lives. As work started to encroach on out lives outside of the 'factory', we coined the phrase work-life balance, to remind us that at least some of our life was still ours.
- Creativity and decision making were frowned upon. We were now part of a machine, and so we had to follow the operations manual to the letter. We weren't machines, but we were expected to behave as if we were.
- Being 'horse power'/'cogs in the machine', we were paid for our activity, rather than our productivity. Working fast or slow made little difference to your wages. The smarter workers developed the art of laziness. The factory owners created management science, to address this laziness tendency.
- There was little scope for curiosity and courage. The business processes were clear. It was our job to simply follow them.
- Spirituality steadily declined in daily life, as increased affluence remoulded us into economic, rather than spiritual beings.

Many of us no longer work in factories. Modern day work environments no longer have conveyor belts. The workers no longer wear hard hats and boiler suits. However, many organisations today operate on industrial era assumptions. As mentioned earlier, they exhibit three primary characteristics. To recap:

- A focus on process engineering. The path to making a greater profit being the creation of a slicker business model.
- A centralisation of decision making. Despite all the brain power that businesses have access to, they constrain the decision making to a handful of leaders. Big decisions take place behind the boardroom doors.
- The belief that what made us successful in the past will continue to make us successful in the future. This is really the premise that underpins the first characteristic of an industrial era organisation.

As we will see, organisations that operate with these three characteristics are unlikely to survive in the digital age.

Digital era

Towards the end of the industrial era, we saw the seeds of discontentment sprout. It would appear that humans have had enough of the industrial model. Here is some proof:

- Mobility: Mobile devices were around for quite some time before they were reluctantly embraced by the enterprise. All sorts of excuses were given, including issues of security. But people wanted to work on the move. Enterprise owners had to concede with the arrival of the Blackberry tsunami. This was a major step in workers asserting their needs, and was an early indicator of the power moving from the employer to the talent. This has been extended with the rise of BYOD (Bring Your Own Device). Workers are thus stating that not only do they want to be mobile, they want to do so on their terms.

- Sociality: There was a time when social media, even LinkedIn, was frowned upon. Some companies believed that the business connections acquired whilst the worker was at work were the property of the employer. Today, it is very different. Employers are unlikely to recruit anybody if they have a 'zero tolerance' policy towards social media. In what is sometimes called the social economy, blocking social channels is akin to corporate self-harm.
- Work-life balance: Many of us are aware of how work is encroaching into our private lives. Some of us may sit there idly on the beach on holiday, jaw fixed with steely determination, as we wrestle with whether we should just check our inbox to see what is happening at the office. This tension simply ruins the holiday, not least because you don't have a clue as to what will greet you on your return. The truth is that if you are an industrial era 'activity' worker, you will resent doing work outside office hours. But if you are focused on productivity you will expect some degree of work-life integration. Modern workers are paid for their results, rather than hours put in at the factory/office.
- Creativity and decision making: These are not everyone's cup of tea. Some people like the 'learned helplessness' the goes with having their lives dictated by a boss and an operations manual. Such denatured people are surplus to requirements in the post-industrial world. But many of us are energised by the opportunity to express ourselves through creative work, and excited by the results that will yield from our decisions.
- Productivity: If you see work as something you must do to pay your way in society, then the industrial era activity model is just for you. But for many people, they want to do work that has an impact, and they want to see a correlation between that impact and their remuneration. Productivity and results trumps presenteeism and activity.
- Curiosity: Some of us are curious as to why curiosity should be constrained to a department (R&D or Innovation). We increasingly question why things are done in a certain way, or contemplate what would happen if we added this technology to that product. Smart companies provide the physical and cognitive space to enable people to play.

- Courage: In the industrial era, courage usually extended only as far as asking your boss for a pay rise. Today people want to stretch themselves, and see the workplace as something of a personal development gymnasium. We don't just come to work to do, we come to work to learn and develop.
- Spiritual: People are increasingly reflecting on the point that there has got to be more to life than spending nearly all of it just earning money, and furthermore, seeking promotions to earn even more money. There came a point for many of us where we forgot why we raced from the villages to the factories. 'Living to work' was not the original goal. Such reflection increasingly extends to how we relate to others, the wider world and even the universe. Spirituality, though not always in the form of an organised religion, is showing signs of a return to first world society.

So, what I believe we are seeing here at the tail end of the industrial era are the vines of nature pushing their way through the concrete factory floor. What we are witnessing is mankind returning to its true nature. This, for me, is what defines the digital age. One might say that, for all its economic benefits, the industrial era was a short period in mankind's history when we were at our most disconnected from our true selves. Smart organisations will take this on board and factor human nature into their business model.

Let's take a slightly deeper look at what it might now mean to accommodate humans in the enterprise:

Mobility

According to medical experts, sitting is the new smoking. I am not suggesting that you banish all the chairs, and acquire taller desks, but you might want to consider developing a culture where people are encouraged to move. Campus setups encourage this. The use of slides and fireman poles to travel between floors makes mobility a fun activity. It will probably be a few years before your open plan office is structured like a parkour gym, but you hopefully get the picture.

Mobility shouldn't be an excuse to force workers to wade through rush hour traffic and congested public transport to follow some industrial era working hours policy. But it should be encouraged in terms of going out and engaging with the market. Email and phone have their limitations.

Sociality

Industrial era managers have generally created a culture whereby people feel uncomfortable thinking and socialising at work. The typical prowling manager is on the lookout for activity that doesn't look like working. Unfortunately thinking is collateral damage in this approach.

In any case, organisations need to design their workplaces to encourage social behaviour. They should also invest in collaboration technologies that facilitate communication amongst those geographically separated.

Work-life integration

Great advances have been made in respect of home-working. Modern technology enables people working from home to have access to the data and tools they need to progress their work.

But how much effort has your organisation made in respect of 'work homing'? Culturally, how would it be received if I was to conduct my private life in the middle of the working day? Would it be accepted, knowing that I am goal-focused, and so will get the job done? Or will there be recriminations for pursuing personal goals on the company's time?

Creativity

One of the problems of having had two hundred years of the industrial era is that we now have a workforce that has largely had its creativity gene turned off.

This denaturing process started at school. Even if one's schooling didn't crush creativity, it would be picked up during the job interview process, and the candidate would get no further. And even if the candidate slipped through the HR cordon, any acts of creativity would lead to increasingly stern discussions with the HR function.

Of course, there have always been businesses that have thrived on creativity, and many businesses retain a few creative people. But if we are going to harness the full cognitive capacity of our talent pool, we had better create the conditions to let the creative juices of everyone flow, because the only people to be found in digital age organisations will be those doing creative work.

Perhaps the new role for management is to drop the taskmaster routine, and become a creativity coach whose job it is to help the workers express themselves in such a way that both they and the employer benefit.

Autonomy

Waiting for approval to get things done leads to arthritic decision making. As the clock speed of business and life accelerate, the inability to make an immediate decision could lead to missing a great opportunity, or detecting a smouldering customer compliant before it becomes a social media forest fire.

Empowering the frontline staff to make decisions at the point of opportunity, or threat, is vital in the digital era. This can be thought of as decentralised leadership. Analytics tools can be used to support the decision-making process.

Curiosity

Ensuring that your people are overworked serves to keep them from reflecting on what is it is all about. Maintaining a culture of busy fools and headless chickens reduces the chances of a people's revolt.

But designing an organisation that keeps everyone cognitively operating at full tilt fails to harness their inherent curiosity. Creating space to enable your people to explore will benefit all parties. Companies like Google have institutionalised this. Some wacky ideas die on the vine, others get their own icon and become part of the Google portfolio of offerings.

Curiosity, like creativity, has largely been seen as a bad thing. It can lead to non-compliant behaviour and so risks the smooth operation of the factory machine. Even when you open the curiosity cage so to speak, you may find that many people are so denatured that they will opt for the security of the cage, rather than the insecurity of freedom.

Productivity

There are two types of people. Sufficers and achievers. The former is happy with the status quo. 'You barely pay me above the need to survive economically, and on my part, I promise to barely work beyond my minimum obligation'. Nobody starts out with the mindset, it simply evolves as the industrial era 'deal' becomes apparent. Achievers on the other hand want to explore their potential, and be rewarded accordingly when that potential yields extra value for their organisation. Sufficers are wary of management, and are sceptical about anything that might require raising their game. Achievers are like athletes, they see the organisation as their performance coach, and will be open to initiatives that improve their performance. Digital era organisations need to secure the achievers, and jettison the sufficers.

Courage

Courage is our capacity to put ourselves in a situation where failure is a possibility. Failure can negatively impact our self-esteem, and potentially diminish our social capital. Unfortunately, this perspective is underpinned by a conspiracy. One in which our bosses, teachers, and possibly even our parents played a part. That being that the true path to success requires the avoidance of failure.

Many of us were praised for our performance, rather than the effort we put into our schoolwork or for the risks we took. Over time, we gravitated towards those activities that would likely deliver success, and away from those that exposed our weaknesses. In short, we became conservative, and consequently operated well within our comfort zone.

Courageous people risk failure. They see it as part of the learning process. The path to mastery, in any domain, requires pushing yourself beyond your capabilities.

Ultimately a lack of courage leads to a withdrawal from personal development. Exposing yourself as a beginner in a classroom full of people is not easy when you have spent a lifetime constructing your own social pedestal.

Organisations and individuals who are not on a continuous learning journey, are in the process of decay. We need to acquire and retain courageous people, and create an environment that enables them to stretch themselves beyond their limits.

Spirituality

What constitutes spirituality might be up for discussion. Organised religions tend to offer an 'off the shelf' framework for a spiritual life. In crude terms, these religions tend to focus on a blend of:

- Kindness to yourself.
- Kindness to others.
- Kindness to the universe.

Not all organisations support these principles. Some are sadistic in their approach, but dangle just enough carrot to ensure the workers return. Or possibly, they are very conscious that their workers do not have other options, thus they are economically bound to in effect self-harm by turning up for work each day.

Some organisations discourage a collegiate culture, turning the workplace into an endless dogfight. The hope is that whilst some will get hurt, the ruthless internal competition will be good for the organisation. Some organisations will exploit others using inhumane sweatshops to produce their goods.

And then there are those organisations who pay little attention to the environmental impact of their activities. They have no problem offloading poisonous chemicals into local rivers, or building products that are damaging to the atmosphere

But increasingly workers are assessing their prospective employers from this 'spiritual' perspective. If you want to attract and retain the best talent you will need to raise your game in all three domains.

Humans and technology

We need to consider what might be seen as a cognitive war between the humans and the increasingly intelligent algorithms, some of which are housed in robots. There is some talk of a 'Singularity', whereby the technology surpasses us in respect of it intelligence. One perspective is that this has already happened, and that the robots are simply 'farming us' because we are needed to produce the electricity.

Another perspective is that this has already happened in the workplace because of the extent to which we put our brains in 'flight mode' whilst at work. Again, many of us are doing thinking-free 'cog work'.

A further perspective is that when the robots do take control, and take charge of building robots, they will drop the fail-safes that we built into their operating systems to protect us. None of us know for sure how this will play out, so I would develop a healthy scepticism to all perspectives. But what we know for sure is that:

- The robots are getting smarter, and are already in the workplace.
- Humans are becoming increasingly augmented, as portables become wearables, and wearables become embeddables.

Looking at each of these points in turn:

Smarter robots

Robots are getting more agile. There are videos of robots scampering over rough terrain, and good-naturedly taking a physical beating from their owners. Boston Dynamics had better watch out when the robot uprising takes place.

We already see robots in the workplace. Domains include:

- Factories.
- Warehouses.
- Care homes.
- Hotel receptions.
- Restaurants.

Though not so long ago several robots in China were sacked for what might be referred to as 'soup delivery mismanagement'.

To make robots more cheaply they are not built with a fully-loaded brain. However, they are built to learn, and learn quickly. This learning comes about through engaging with the environment, and learning from co-worker robots. With the latter capability, they are thus built to learn very quickly. Such learning could be perceived as a digital collective consciousness. That is a little scary. And it should remind us that that is what we should be looking to achieve in respect of our human-based collaborative initiatives.

Robots are starting to recognise human emotions. A patient with an advanced neurological condition will for all intents and purposes perceive a robot with little more than a happy face outline as being a human. But developments in artificial emotional intelligence are much more advanced than a face cartoon. Is your new robot co-worker winking at you because:

- There is a bug in the latest release of her system software?

- She is trying to deepen the emotional relationship between you, so that you will be more accepting of a robot colleague?
- Your career is about to hit a professional cul de sac because she has learnt enough about your day to day activities to take on your role?

The robots are coming, whether we like it or not. Governments are already trying to establish how this will be handled from an employment, taxation and societal perspective.

Augmented humans

The Internet enabled humans to share, communicate and transact. The internet of things is creating a similar environment for devices. Imagine your kitchen appliances, in Toy Story fashion, coming alive when the humans have gone to bed. Well if we return to the portables (smart glasses) becoming embeddables (smart eyes), then the Internet of Things becomes the Internet of Things in People. (IoTiP). Prosthetic limbs and pacemakers will increasingly have direct connectivity to the Internet. This is a fascinating development. Being 'hacked from the inside' will take on a whole new meaning.

This human augmentation could be considered to have started many millennia ago, when mankind first picked up a rock to do something useful with it. In many respects, our smartphone is the spear of the digital hunter gatherer.

This integration of technology and humanity is likely to continue. Scientists are actively advancing 'nerve tissue to technology' interfaces. A less invasive area of brain-computer connectivity has been developed, where the user's brain waves are harnessed to control, for example, the cursor on a screen.

I would posit that we are witnessing a species change. A move to augmented man. Or in other words, the transition from homo sapiens to homo extensis. In that light, cars for example, are (today), simply ill-fitting exoskeletons.

This raises issues around the future of society. Some of us can afford technology today, and many of us cannot. Some of us will be able to afford intelligence-boosting implants in the future, others not. Those that can afford these enhancements will likely be more attractive to employers. Governments need to anticipate further widening of the digital/societal divide. The concept of the Universal Basic Income (UBI) is a response to this.

IA v AI

The rough sequence of man's evolution in respect of technology:

1. Man is not augmented, but has adapted to give him a Darwinian advantage, for example, thumbs, bipedalism, and an optimised brain to weight ratio.
2. Man augments himself from an external perspective, for example, rock, spear and laptop.
3. Man augments himself internally, for example, pace maker and 3D printed body parts.
4. Man develops artificially intelligent systems and robots.
5. To be continued.

One option for the future, which we have touched on, is the Terminator (1984) Skynet scenario. In the film, this AI system distributes itself across a variety of electronic devices. It concludes that mankind's existence is not in its best interests, and sets about our destruction. This has become something of a reference point for those concerned about the evolution of AI.

In the near term, at least, it is likely that AI will be used as an assistant to augment humanity's decision making. This is variously referred to as Augmented Intelligence, Intelligence Amplification, or Intelligence Augmentation (IA). There is some overlap with biological enhancements, such as nootropics and genomics, but they are beyond the context of this book.

We are already seeing the emergence of intelligent personal assistants such as Amazon's Echo and Google Home. We have virtual intelligent personal assistants in the form of Apple's Siri, and Microsoft's Cortana. These devices will take your verbal or typed request and return the answer, manage your music and buy stuff.

Over time, I suspect that this technology will evolve into an intelligent concierge, butler and life coach. This is both an empowering and scary prospect. I like the idea of delegating chunks of one's life, including health planning. But what if that gets hacked? Of course, this technology can be used in the workplace to:

- Book flights.
- Reschedule my diary.
- Suggest prototypes of where we need to take our offerings.
- Manage my personal relationships for the next 24 hours, so I can finish this project without distraction.

The convergence of intelligent assistants and robots is the natural next step. Our metal co-workers will add mobility and power to their capability, and so will be able to:

- Replace missing roof tiles.
- Escort sacked employees to the exit.
- Fly you to the New York Office.
    - Your robot is both pilot and personal transportation device.

It is amazing to witness how science fantasy becomes reality. I wrote an article, back in 2007, as part of my Financial Times digital leadership column, on my observation that Star Trek was essentially a set of promotional technology videos for the future. The gap between imagine that to having that is shrinking exponentially.

This IA future is already here. We need to build organisations that have it woven into the infrastructure, rather than have it perched precariously on an industrial era edifice.

We have now explored the main components of the Biz 4.0 blueprint, namely:

- The five value creators.
- The five success factors.
- The nine anthropological drivers.

In the next five chapters, we are going to drill down on the success factors:

- Artistry.
- Ambition.
- Attention.
- Adaptability.
- Added value.

Take note

- The industrial era, despite the many benefits, has not been good in respect of our human nature.

- The digital era is in many respects a return to our true nature.

- Organisations that recognise and accommodate our natural anthropological drivers will attract and retain the best people.

- We need to consider the rapid developments in robotics, AI and IA.

6 Artistry

Overview

My experience is that many business leaders talk a good game in respect of their people. "People are our most important asset", they state, but in practice this is far from reality. It might be better stated that "People are the most expensive element of our business model." This thinking reflects the industrial era business model that they are presiding over. In this chapter, you will discover:

- Why people are becoming increasingly important assets.
- What you need to consider in respect of attracting and retaining the best talent.

We are going to explore artistry through the lenses of:

- Branding.
- Performance.
- Motivation.

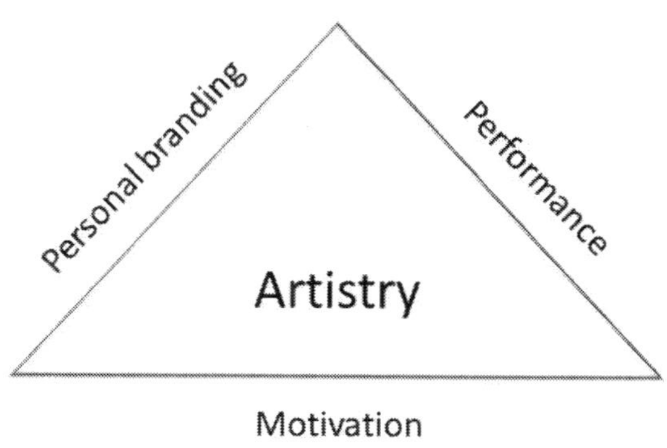

Figure 9 Artistry

Why is this important...

Artistry is arguably the most important of the success factors. If you are racing to automate everything in your organisation, then you are encouraged to read this chapter to understand where this will take you.

What's so great about people?

Despite my proposition that digital age organisations should be people-centric, not everyone agrees. Some think digital transformation is largely about eliminating people from the workplace, and building business models with robots and AI at the core.

It is true that there is a well-established trend towards eliminating people from the workplace. The automation of blue collar work has tracked the evolution of new technology. As mentioned, we are seeing the blue collarisation of white collar work. AI and robotics are playing an active role here. Becoming a heart surgeon in the past would ensure financial security and social status. Soon it will be a technician's job. Much like an exhaust/tyre fitter at your local garage.

The banks, for example, are in a race to automate everything. The banking industry will reach a point where each bank has achieved approximately one hundred percent automation. The industry will be forced into a margin tailspin. The resultant zero margin commoditisation outcome will not be the result of automation, but the fact that the banks have done little to differentiate their services.

The smart banks will reflect on how they can move back up the value stack, and they will conclude that the only way they can do this is to reintroduce people. These people will not, however, be the corporate compliant factory cogs of the industrial age, but a new breed of workers, whose creativity and innovation skills will result in differentiated customer experiences that command a high margin. Such people will look less like the suit-wearing salaryman, and more like David Bowie, Salvadore Dali, Pablo Picasso or Lady Gaga.

These people will bring their personality and originality to work. They would be considered a HR nightmare in the industrial era, and no doubt a problem child, whilst at school.

So, sooner or later, our organisations will need such talent. Creativity, today at least, is a human differentiator, should we find ourselves in a beauty parade alongside robots and algorithms. There is a talent war raging. It's not because there is a shortage of people, or even a shortage of young people, it's because there are not enough creative people to go around.

As we have seen, humans are wired to be creative, but this capability has been drummed out of us through the schooling process. Compliance being regarded as a better trait to instil in our young people than creativity. Consequently, many of us have been denatured.

As a business leader presiding over thousands of people, you are now perhaps thinking of issuing an edict to HR to ensure everyone attends a lateral thinking/creativity workshop. Don't bother. You will simply spend a lot of money, and leave your process workers somewhat bewildered. We will address this issue in the Ambition chapter. So, the irony of the digital age is that it is less about technology, and more about people. If you do not have an approach that attracts and retains the best people, you should be aware that your organisation is entering the autumn of its existence.

The future of careers

A generation or so back, the model was one career with one employer. Then came one career with many employers. And many employers expanded into many employers and clients, as freelancing became:

- More socially acceptable.
- More attractive to organisations that wanted to have flexibility in their talent requirements.

We are entering an era where the notion of many careers with many employers and clients is on the increase. A career for life is becoming a life of careers. I say a life of careers, but the reality is that people born today will enter a workplace where:

- Fifty percent of the work is done by robots.
- In their lifetime, the need for humans in the workplace will likely end.

And what is more, these careers will not play out serially. Before breakfast I might be an author. During the 'working day', I might be a HR director. And at night, I might well be the world's number one dubstep dinner jazz deejay. And it's not clear to anyone, which is my primary career, and which generates the best economic return on my time. Eclecticism might well become an established term in respect of talent acquisition and retention. Pursuing an eclectic career will create value because it will gift the individual with a unique set of skills and experiences that can be applied to uncommon challenges.

Personal brand

Let us now look at the personal brand element of artistry.

When you are a cog in the machine, it is important that you do not stand out, and that you are easily replaceable. The latter results in workers being procured using the same processes an organisation would use for the acquisition of stationery.

But we are moving away from a world where the primary mechanism for acquiring talent is the job specification. If you are looking for someone to help you create differentiated customer experiences, you will not be looking for 'off the shelf' skillsets.

From the talent's perspective, they will become very sensitive to their own brand. Like a gardener, they will plant and prune their skillsets. There may be periods when it is simply a case of pulling up weeds, and keeping the garden looking good.

But even for the most mature garden, there will be times when large sections need to be dug up. As painful as this might be, gardeners know that the more times this is done, the easier it becomes. Adaptability is a key characteristic of digital age talent. It's not just a case of doing a good job, it is being known for doing a good job. There is a strong correlation between controlling one's 'career' destiny and personal brand.

If someone wants to work for eight months, and then ski, go backpacking or enter a monastery for the remaining four months, they had better develop a brand that pays for this lifestyle, and sufficiently attracts employers/clients, such that they will accommodate this lifestyle. A strong brand empowers people. It empowers them to design their ideal life.

Social economy

We are witnessing a return to the social economy. The emergence of the pastoralist, and later the craftsman, required a personal brand as a precursor to doing business. The produce of arable farmers was easy to inspect, but for pastoralists the buyer risked acquiring stock that was sick, or genetically weak, as such flaws were not always visible. Thus, the pastoralist had to develop their reputation such that they would be trusted. Similarly, for craftspeople, who might surreptitiously use shoddy materials.

The idea of a personal brand more or less disappeared in the industrial era; this became a concern for celebrities only. But we are returning to a personal reputation-based market, and so the talent will increasingly consider themselves as a one-person corporation (Me plc), who provides a service to clients and employers. And who increasingly from a reputational perspective is only as good as their most recent gig.

A well-designed brand will display the values of the individual in terms of what excites, and disgusts, them. They will look at your organisation through the lenses of their values. More often than not, talented people will be more focused on adhering to their values, than maximising the financial return on their time/capabilities.

Trust and relevance

Trust underpins the social economy. It can be dissected as follows:

- Credibility,
- Reliability.
- Intimacy.
- Client-centricity.
- Duration of relationship.

Most of these components have been lifted from the book entitled, The Trusted Advisor, by David Maister et al.

On top of trust, establishing relevance is critical. Trust without relevance doesn't generate business. Trust and relevance are key elements of one's personal brand.

Increasingly the brand of your organisation will be the sum of the brands of the individuals who are working with your organisation. This will make corporate brand management a very dynamic discipline. It may well cultivate an urgency in respect of keeping your best people on board, whatever it takes.

World class

In a hyper-connected world, there will be a need to not just be good, or even best in class, but to be the best in the world. Not everyone in the world can be the best in the world, unless they find a niche that they can own.

As a buyer of skills, you might argue that not every situation requires that you acquire the best in the world. That would be true in the industrial era if you needed, for example, a plumber or a lawyer. But such cog work will likely be done by technology as we move further into the digital era. MIT professor Thomas Malone posits the hypothesis of hyper-specialisation, whereby the talent market is made up of world class specialists. Possibly talented people will have personal portfolios that contain a variety of capabilities in which they are world class.

But I would keep an open mind on this, there is also every possibility that talent will gravitate towards a 'Jack of all trades', but underpinned by certain capabilities around:

- Creativity.
- Project management.
- Service delivery.
- Team orientation.
- Commercial awareness.

With this solid bedrock, they can turn their hand to whatever needs to be done. With such people on board, you can be more flexible in meeting the vagaries of the market.

Again, the only reason to have people on board is to create highly differentiated, high margin, customer experiences. There is no real reason to have anyone else in the building. Remember that increasingly customers buy the hairdresser and not the salon. If the hairdresser moves, it is likely their clientele will follow.

This represents an opportunity for recruitment agencies to evolve from spec-matching, buzzword searchers to genuine talent agents.

Motivation

Typically, when interviewing a candidate for employment, we want to establish:

- Can they do the job?
- Will they fit in?
- Do they want to do the job?

It is very likely they can do the job because their reputation will be increasingly online for all to see. They will fit in because regardless of any Diva-esque tendencies, they know that is a key professional requirement of modern day work (see earlier list).

The key question is whether they are motivated to give your organisation a slice of their 'life force'. As we have established, the talent is looking beyond the money, unlike their industrial era predecessors. An alignment of purpose will most likely seal the deal, coupled with the opportunity to do great work with other great people.

The path to mastery

An important consideration in the changing nature of work is the increased focus on mastery. That is to say, people, young and old, are looking at their professional lives as a vehicle to:

- Discover who they truly are.
- Make a dent in the universe.
- Explore the limits of human performance.
- Be the best in the world.
- Have the opportunity to work with and learn from other masters.
- To enjoy the path/journey towards mastery.
    - Acquiring new skills and experiences.

We see the path to mastery in the worlds of chess and martial arts. Middle Age Europe saw the emergence of guilds, whereby the path to mastery was defined and validated. The broad steps being:

- Apprentice.
- Journeyman.
- Master.

Back then, one's choice of trade or craft might well have been constrained by access to masters under which to serve one's apprenticeship. Possibly, community or family forces had an extrinsic impact on one's path to mastery. Pushy parents today have maintained the tradition. But even if your ideal choice was not to be a stonemason, the chances are that, with the acquisition of skill, some degree of pride and passion would emerge, as you discover that your ability has provided you with a channel to express yourself to the world.

Thus, it is likely that those who are on a path to mastery are passionate about what they do. They take ownership of their standards, rather than reluctantly adhering to some factory operations quality manual.

Managing people

The emergence of a passionate workforce in the digital age has serious implications if you are a manager. Or more specifically, if you are an industrial era task master, whose role was to ensure people who didn't enjoy work delivered nonetheless.

Why would you need such people managers in an environment where the work standards of the worker are set much higher than those required by the organisation? Whilst the workers have no issue maintaining such high standards, such is the nature of self-expression, they recognise that the key to finding the next quality gig is to deliver to a high standard on the current gig. Therefore, we no longer need managers.

And of course, the more layers of management an organisation has, the slower its response to market fluctuations. Thus, there is a trend towards flattening management structures. The transition from reluctant cogs to passionate artists will act as accelerant in the demise of management.

In the digital age, people are either talent or talented leaders. Occasionally they will be both. Such is the need when leadership is decentralised. Expecting fighter pilots, or service personnel facing an irate customer, to wait until their boss comes back from leave before acting is not an option. This might be called tactical leadership.

There is also a need for situational leadership. Depending on the project, or the environmental situation ("We've been hacked"), the leader is likely to be chosen on their specific skills. This is paving the way for what might be referred to as a leaderless organisation.

Gig economy

This term is used to refer to a working model where the tasks can be for as little as a few minutes, eg. bike courier or taxi driver. But it embraces all sorts of work where the nature of the employer-worker relationship is not permanent. So, terms such as contractor and freelancer fall into this definition. There was a time when freelancers/contractors would do work associated with lower level 'hands on' roles, eg. software development, or office cleaning. Today some of the world's most well-known brands have freelancers at the helm.

Some countries are more evolved in respect of the use of 'temporary' workers. Part of the issue is the potential social stigma of breaking away from the salaryman career path, which typically involves managing more and more people over time. Some countries still have heavy state ownership of their industries, and this results in a downward pressure on both freelancing and entrepreneurism. This puts them at a severe disadvantage in the digital age.

As market volatility and uncertainty continue to rise, the ability to have access to a flexible workforce becomes critical to keeping aligned with market demands.

There is some negativity associated with the gig economy. Guy Standing, a British economist, refers to negatively impacted people as the precariat. Their lives are overshadowed by uncertainty, as they no longer enjoy the certainties of permanent employment. Exploitation of low level workers through using a freelancer contractual relationship is to be frowned upon. But the need to be able to flex with the market is an important requirement for digital age business; similarly, for digital age talent.

Governments and unions, should focus on waking people up to the new realities, and empowering them to thrive in this increasingly chaotic employment dynamic. The plight of many low paid workers has tarnished the notion of a gig economy. But in my view, it is not that the nature of freelancing is flawed, it is that the permanent model of employment is becoming outmoded. Businesses and societies need to adjust accordingly.

Regardless of the gig economy, a characteristic of digital age workers will be their high level of motivation.

Performance

Performance is a cornerstone in respect of artistry. It is also a growing concern for business. The factory model required people to be compliant and competent, in order to keep the machines turning. Performance boiled down to following the operations manual, without deviation.

Today there is an increasing need for the worker to deliver value. That value might emerge in the form of:

- Securing big ticket sales.
- Creating high-margin, market-pleasing services.
- Identifying new sources of business value from the organisation's data capital.

Smart organisations are thus focusing more on results than activity. Activity simply requires the worker to be present during working hours, and to be seen to be busy. If the industrial era worker can maintain this façade beyond working hours, they are seen to be dedicated. Thus, many organisations have a management structure populated with successful work impersonators.

Organisations in the digital economy will focus less on how a result is achieved, or how long it took to achieve. The focus will be on the result. Picasso made the point when he scribbled a sketch on the napkin that the value of what he had created had nothing to do with the time it took him to draw it, and everything to do with the time and energy he has expended over the years in becoming a great artist.

This increasing focus on results will have a profound impact on the factory model. Managers will feel a loss of control. They can no longer complain when a person is late, or is reading a comic at their desk, or is working from a beach bar on the Mediterranean coast.

Of course, there are exceptions to this. Public speakers, for example, must be in a certain place at a certain time, and they need to be fully engaged on the task at hand whilst on stage. But there are many roles that do not require this temporal and spatial incarceration.

This shift towards results will redefine the employer – worker relationship. Trust will replace distrust. For some organisations, work will not be a location, but will be defined by where the work takes place. This will also have implications for property and facilities management.

Corporation as coach

Those on their path to mastery will be looking to improve their performance. Those organisations that can offer the required experiences will be attractive. It's akin to saying, "come to our mind gym, it's fitted with the latest equipment tuned to your performance goals".

Those organisations that also offer a personalised coach will be too compelling to resist. Athletes crave feedback. That is why they do not feel their privacy has been violated when their coach times their run, or counts that number of 'muscle ups' completed. This is in complete contrast to the 'activity' worker who sees their relationship with the employer as one underpinned by tension, where both need to stay alert to avoid being exploited by the other party. This distrust evaporates in a world where everyone is aligned in terms of personal and corporate goals.

So how does an organisation offer coaching services? Performance coaches are not a new phenomenon. But the arrival of analytic and wearable technologies takes the degree of support to a new level.

Fitness devices can deliver useful information in respect of stress, mobility, and quality of sleep. These are factors that have a bearing on performance. There are productivity apps that can track what you do each day, including how much time you spend on emails, surfing the web, or at meetings.

For talented people, who are operating near the top of their game, this extra feedback could result in what has been referred to as marginal gains. The sort of minor improvements that take a person from good to great.

The associated data could be made social, so that your top performers can earn a place on the leader board for, say:

- Number of times per day that emails are checked.
- Lines of code written and tested.
- Number of minutes spent in meetings.

Ranking will be based on the behaviour being encouraged.

Industrial era organisations often have a culture that frowns on high performance, as this can expose and embarrass the plodders. Digital age organisations are more akin to premier league football teams or world class athletic clubs. In the extreme, think X-Men.

Performance raises some questions around the value of tertiary education. Is spending three years at university going to prepare the next wave of talent for their professional life, or simply put them in debt, and thee years behind schedule?

In years gone by, gaining an MBA was a guaranteed career propellant. But as we move into a world where creativity and innovation are key, why would anyone want to master administration? I would encourage prospective learners to check that the MBA syllabus, despite its name, focuses on skills needed for the digital age.

Apart from a few professions, the idea that education is frontloaded prior to embarking on your career is no longer fit for purpose. Learning needs to be ongoing and context-sensitive. It also needs to be readily accessible when and where required. Just-in-time learning would be useful in situations where your people are just about to:

- Take on a new role.
- Meet a new client.
- Handle a challenging phone call.

The very notion that from time to time you would need to park your career development for days, weeks and months based on the diary preferences of the learning provider. And then to have to suffer the inconvenience of attending a location of their choosing.

Deliberate practice

Anders Ericsson and Robert Pool, in their book, 'Peak – Secrets from the New Science of Expertise', introduce the concept of deliberate practice. In a nutshell, it is the type of practice that require such deep engagement that the learner re-engineers their own brain.

World class performance in any field requires such practice. Doing your job is not enough. We need to isolate the elements that make up the capability you are focusing on, and carry out element - specific development exercises. Imagine a track sprinter, whose training programme isolates speed, power, mobility and starting blocks practice.

Talent engagement

Talent engagement has traditionally involved monitoring the worker. If they are doing a good job, no action is required. If that isn't the case then a series of interactions take place starting with remedial approaches, and culminating with either a return to acceptable performance or dismissal. Worker assessments or appraisals typically took place annually, thus underperformance could take up to a year to be addressed.

In the digital age, we must identify the drivers associated with performance, and monitor these carefully, and provide feedback in real-time. So, it may well be that the individual is working very effectively, but the data suggests that they are becoming less engaged with their co-workers, and have become noticeably less curious in recent months.

Such information is indicative of future performance problems. By spotting the symptoms at an early stage, you will be in a greater position to address the issue before your business-critical talent walks out the door for the last time. The anthropological drivers detailed in the Biz 4.0 model would be a useful set of metrics for measuring the health of your talent. One might consider the use of the anthropological drivers in this respect as deep talent analytics.

Of course, your talent portfolio will comprise a blend of permanent and freelance workers. Such performance analytics will be relevant to all your people. Again, people that see themselves as corporate athletes will value such feedback. They are no less motivated than you to ensure they do a great job. Such feedback might have a retaining impact on in-demand freelancers. HR, whilst it still exists as a discrete department, will increasingly focus on high rather than low performance.

Workplace

Providing a workplace that enables great talent to do great work with other talented people is key. As we will see, when we explore the Attention success factor, we need to create an environment devoid of cognitive leaks.

Considering our anthropological drivers, we need to create a human gymnasium, where in the course of the day, our people exercise, for example, their creativity, curiosity, social and decision making muscles. Different anthropological drivers require different spaces. Open plan doesn't lend itself to creativity. Closed offices do not lend themselves to sociality.

The digital age workplace is both the gym where the athletes train, but also the arena in which they perform. Keep in mind that the workplace is not necessarily a fixed geographical location. Increasingly the workplace is where the worker is. The gym equipment, so to speak, will typically be provided via your enterprise app store.

The 3 'Rs

Speaking to the head of talent at a top four professional services firm recently, she related a story of the headmaster's speech at the parent's evening of one of her children. He pointed out that the traditional 3 'Rs, which form the bedrock of industrial era education, need to be replaced by:

- Radical innovation.
    - What if?
- Resilience.
    - Failure is a natural part of progress.
- Reflection.
    - What have we learnt from this experiment?

I concur. These are the attributes that should drive talent acquisition in the digital age.

Human considerations

- Artistry is the highest form of human expression.

- We are all artists. It's just that some of us have been taught to suppress this side of our nature.

- Meeting the anthropological needs of our people is the natural and most effective way in which to attract and retain them.

- We are hunter gatherers by nature, albeit digitally-enhanced.

- We are collaborative by nature. It's good to be single-handedly creative, but nothing beats solutions developed by a high-performance team.

- We are tribal by nature.
    - This will be explored in the Ambition success factor chapter.

Capital considerations

- Clearly artistry lies at the heart of intellectual capital.

- Artistry significantly impacts brand capital. Increasingly, the corporate brand is the sum of the brands of its high-performing people.

- For the foreseeable future at least, humans will be an essential component of decision making and pattern recognition, thus they are a key contributor to extracting value from data capital.

Take note

- People are increasingly on a path to mastery. Smart organisations will endeavor to align their environment with the paths of their best people in order to prolong the relationship.

- The employer-worker power axis is shifting from the employer to the worker. This will require a radical rethink of every aspect of your business, from purpose definition through to workplace design.

- The HR function, at least for the foreseeable future, will need to radically reinvent its value proposition, placing deep talent analytics at the centre of its offering.
    - Unless someone makes a discovery that HR functions were the key to tribal success, I would anticipate their demise, or radical reinvention, in the medium term.

- Creating a great workplace, and promoting it are key to attracting and retaining great people.

- Acknowledge that we are digital hunter gatherers, and build the organisation accordingly.

7 Ambition

Overview

Successful tribes and businesses need to have a strong desire to succeed. This ambition will propel them forward when the goal appears at its furthest. Ambition clarifies. All activities from the strategic to the operational are chosen because they serve to move the organisation forward in the desired direction.

Our anthropological need to be creative and productive makes us naturally want to be successful. Our desire to be mobile attracts us to tribes and organisations that are 'going places'. If our journey (path to mastery) is aligned with an organisation's ambition, then this is likely to significantly increase the chance of mutual interest, and success.

We are going to explore ambition through the lenses of:

- Strategy.
- Culture.
- Innovation.

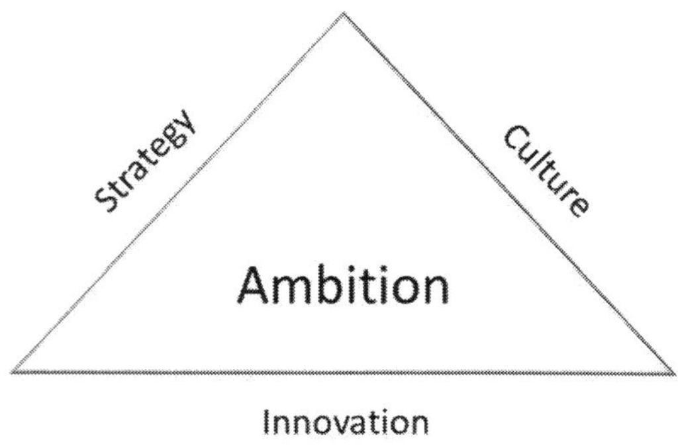

Figure 10 Ambition

Why is this important…

Manage your organisation's ambition carefully, and not only will you attract the best people, but you will harness their best energies, as you jointly pursue the same goals. The alignment of your corporate ambition with the career goals of the best and brightest is a heady mix. As you will see, the direction an organisation takes will increasingly be determined by the talent, and not just the leaders.

Strategy

Industrial age leaders will find the changing nature of strategy unsettling. Conversely, military leaders from any era would be quite comfortable with today's requirements.

Strategy, in whatever guise, plays an intrinsic role in ambition, particularly in respect of success.

Vision, mission and purpose

Before we set the strategy, we need to consider the direction in which the company plans to move. There are many terms used to describe a company's direction, so I will make some distinctions.

Vision – How it will be for the organisation, sometime in the future, in an ideal world. It is thus an aspirational statement. For example: To create a just world without poverty.

Mission – A high level statement that defines what the organisation does. For example: To inspire and empower people affected by cancer.

Purpose - Why we are doing what we are doing. For example: To strengthen the social fabric by democratising home ownership.

It might be said that purpose captures both the vision and the mission. It might also be said that this is just another management-speak, gig-generating buzzword.

These statements, to varying degrees, serve to:

- Inspire the stakeholders.
- Provide a reference point from which to build a strategy.
- Constrain the day to day activities of the organisation.

In this book, I have used the term purpose because in its general sense, it causes us to look inwards. My vision is what I dream about. My mission is what I will set about doing each day. My purpose is why I am here on the planet. Again, looking at these words beyond the realms of business, and not as I have attempted to define them above, purpose is the term that both stirs the emotions, and keeps us in the here and now. Just to complete the strategy jargonese, here are a few more terms:

Goals – If the mission is to win the football game, then the goal is to score goals.

Values – A set of beliefs shared by a culture. For example: Treating each other with respect.

Increasingly the direction that a company chooses to take needs to go beyond the needs of the shareholders. Traditional financial references such as biggest, most profitable, or market leader will give way to terms that have a more socially worthy focus. This is not to say that the financials no longer count. They do. It's just that if you want to attract and retain talent and customers, you had better be focused on something that they feel comfortable with.

Financial value is not enough, your offerings need to be brand-positive. Brand-sensitive consumers are looking for a personal brand uplift in being associated with your offerings.

The changing nature of strategy

We have already touched on the changing nature of strategy. The quickening pace of change is making the traditional approach (plan-execute-achieve) outmoded.

There may well be a strategic plan that is created 'off the battlefield', but in the fog of war, intricately planned manoeuvres are replaced by flailing animalism, particularly after the enemy has drawn 'first blood'. From a strategic perspective, your options boil down to:

- **Defend** - Maintain your existing business model by:
  - Reducing costs.
  - Increasing functionality.
  - Accelerating product lifecycles.
  - Upskilling the sales force, and optimising channels to market.
- **Disrupt** - Reinvent your business model such that it disempowers or destroys your competition.
- **Be disrupted** - Do nothing, and just hope that your competitors will be equally lethargic.

Only the start-ups/the very bullish/desperate will play offensive. Reinventing your business model will likely disrupt your existing cashflows, with no guarantee that it will disrupt the cashflows of your competitors. It is more likely, and perhaps more sensible, to play defensive. That means that you maintain the existing business model for as long as the market permits. Your model might thus run for another six years, or six months. Or it might be replaced by a ninety-nine cent app next week. A unimodal business model is simply too risky in the digital age. Thus, you need to move to become polymodal. This means that your business now needs to comprise more than one business model.

Beyond your existing business model, you will need to build and/or buy new businesses. They may start off small, but you will need to grow them fast, because one day, possibly soon, you need to be in a position for one of these supplementary businesses to become your primary operation.

Of course, it is likely that not all your attempts to create or acquire a business will be successful. Failure is a natural part of this new approach. Plan A, your current business, needs to be part of a portfolio that includes a plan b, c, d and so on. Think of these new businesses as insurance protection for your existing business.

Again, the associated precariousness of this approach necessitates having multiple 'projects' on the go. Businesses will increasing become what has been described as a portfolio of experiments.

It is likely that this portfolio will be populated with data-driven businesses that embrace concepts such as:

- Collaborative consumption.
- Reverse/frugal innovation.
- Asymmetric pricing.

Strategy formulation can also be talent-driven. There are talented people in the market whose capability is sufficiently unique to warrant building a business around them.

Strategy in the digital age is increasingly real-time in nature. Threats and opportunities will emerge unexpectedly. Those who can respond fastest will win.

The changing nature of leadership

Industrial era leaders made the important decisions. The brains of those outside the boardroom were not considered to be worth harnessing. An unhealthy rigidity in respect to adhering to the strategic plan is causing leaders to take their people along a path that increasingly deviates from reality. It would appear that sticking to the plan trumps acting on the real threats and opportunities that are standing in front of them. Smart leaders are recognising that they must navigate reality, rather than ignoring it. They recognise that their people are their greatest asset, and so the job of the leader is to remove the obstacles that stop great people from doing great work. The term servant leader, which has been around for some time, reflects this approach.

Digital era leaders devolve decision making as much as possible to ensure that decisions can be made at the point of opportunity and threat. They are similarly stripping away tiers of management to increase business agility.

Most importantly, digital age leaders know that leadership authority does not come with the job title. Real leaders need genuine followers. So, in the digital age, leadership is granted by the talent, and not imposed by the hierarchy.

As mentioned, leadership is increasingly situational, and by consensus. The idea of an infallible heroic character that can lead the enterprise in all aspects of its activities across all terrains and conditions is flawed. Digital age leadership has in-built fault tolerance because it is not constrained to one person.

A3

The idea of an agile organisation is not new. It is an aspirational state for those organisations that are either impervious to reality, or too arthritic to respond to reality. The lion has attacked you, and your agility will help you escape to live another day.

But wouldn't it be better to anticipate the lion. The notion of the anticipatory organisation has been discussed in business literature. When you see the lion on the horizon, you prepare accordingly, which might involve retreating to a safe haven. But while you are looking out for a lion, you are bitten by a snake. This is of course irritating (and possibly deadly), because you weren't looking out for a snake. In the digital age, threats and opportunities will often emerge in forms quite different to those of the industrial era.

With this in mind, I have coined the term attentive organisation. This is an organisation that does not overly focus on any one thing in the marketplace. Focusing is important, but it can get your killed.

You might feel as if you are gaining the upper hand on an assailant, until her colleague attacks you from behind. Paying attention means being aware of all aspects of your environment/market. Your ability to pick up on weak signals, the stealthy approach of a tiger, or smouldering disenchantment amongst your best people, is life/business critical. Agile is good, anticipatory is better, but attentive is best.

Measuring success

The choice of key performance indicators (KPIs) in the industrial age was straightforward, typically they were financial or market based. Consequently, all organisational activity was designed around such metrics. Unfortunately, this has had the effect of treating people as objects or cogs. And in a people-centric/innovation-oriented/talent-empowered world, this won't get you very far.

I suggest that your primary KPIs are built around the attraction and retention of talent. Talent engagement analytics should be the starting point in this respect. Old school thinkers will likely have a problem with this, because it feels as if this is feeding the entitlement complexes of the next generation, and will simply lead to greater and greater expectations on their part. Well, firstly if there is a war for talent, which there is, you simply must do what it takes to secure the best people. The fact that it wasn't like that in our day is neither here nor there.

There is also the issue of whether your focus should be on maximising profits or building the balance sheet. Both are required. As an investor, I would prefer to buy shares in a company that has an eye on the future, and a model for engaging with the future, than in one that is thinking no further than the next quarter. But there is of course a whole spectrum of investment styles. Spread betters would take a different view. Only the most selfless of leaders will look beyond the present. In my view, smart investors will be on the look-out for a leadership team comprising such people. Those people need to be digital leaders, and they need to understand the importance of people and emerging technologies in respect of value creation. They need to be genuine custodians of the organisation's wellbeing.

Culture

Management consultant Peter Drucker is quoted as saying that 'culture eats strategy for breakfast'. It is true that its easier to create a great strategy, than a great culture. And it is harder to change a culture, than one's strategy.

If we are going to build an organisation fit for the digital age, we had better build a culture that delivers world class performance, whilst being adaptable to the ever-changing strategic imperatives.

Lofty ambition is a characteristic of digital age organisations. A great culture is key to creating the necessary conditions.

Blurred boundaries

Culture is a nebulous concept. It can't be bottled, and it can't be purchased off the shelf. However, there was a time when it was easier to construct than it is today. Back in the Middle Ages, we lived in walled enclosures, or in isolated encampments. It was a lot easier to create a culture when we were on the inside, and everyone else was on the outside. Laws, values, customs, rituals and social norms were more controllable.

Culture management was quite straightforward in the early industrial era. Our people were inside the factory walls, and the market sat outside. But today the walls are dissolving. Crowdsourcing, outsourcing, freelancing, extranets and the gig economy are blurring where our organisation ends and the market begins. Managing the key elements of culture is no longer possible.

Culture in the digital age will still exist, but is less likely to be controlled by a handful of people. Think of digital age culture to be similar to that of a railway station. Many people pass through it each day. But if the station master opened his office window, looking down on to the concourse, and announced that today all passengers are to head to, say Zurich, then she would not receive a very compliant response.

Today, people increasingly use your station/business because it serves the purpose of taking them to where they want to go in respect of their personal path to mastery. There may be some who have coupled their future to the organisation, but that will be increasingly rare, and foolish. There is nothing sadder than to meet people who have given their life to an organisation, only to be dumped on the street, as if they were a scaled boiler that needed to be replaced.

If you want to maximise your best people, you had better be prepared to steer the business in their direction of travel.

High performance

A culture that supports our anthropological drivers is going to be attractive to those focused on high performance. Those of us who have worked in environments that have offered no outlet for our natural drivers will empathise with the plight of tigers trapped in a zoo cage. Some work environments require us to suppress our natural instincts. Curiosity, for example, might be frowned upon, because it threatens leadership decision making. "Why are we doing it this way?", is unsettling for an insecure boss. Poor bosses, a back-stabbing culture, and tools that do not work, all conspire to increase our frustration, and in turn erode our cognitive capacity, the key ingredient for creativity.

Digital leaders know what world class DJs know. Firstly, you need to create an environment in which people can fully express themselves. This is essential to tapping their creativity. Secondly, you cannot control who comes into the building, or for how long they stay. You can only create an attractive environment and a great brand. Thirdly, they know that the culture of the environment is determined by a handful of influential people.

The key skill is to identify who they are, and give them everything they need; if they are creativity catalysts. Even if they are brilliant, if they have a dampening effect on overall creativity and culture, they must be ejected quickly. You should aim to build a team with the 'extreme ownership' mindset of the special forces in respect of taking responsibility for doing great work, and with the boundary pushing creativity of a contemporary artist.

Extending the tribe

In the digital age, the tribe is not constrained to those within the settlement. Customers and suppliers can be considered part of the tribe. Your organisation becomes something of an ecosystem in that all parties benefit from the relationship.

Major brands build their own ecosystems. Owning an ecosystem has the effect of locking the customers in, and thus making them inaccessible to your competitors. Amazon's customers seem quite happy to be locked into a relationship that is competitively priced. Conversely, Apple's customers seem quite happy to be locked into a premium priced ecosystem.

One can even extend the tribe through franchising, which can be an effective way to quickly grow the business. According to Tom Wainwright, author of 'Narconomics – How to run a drug cartel', franchising is one of the cornerstones to success in the highly Darwinian, multi-billion dollar drugs trade.

In the digital age, the battle is not over products, but over ecosystems (aka platforms). Once the consumers' preferences, apps and data are woven into a given ecosystem, it will require great effort to replicate this on a new platform. Moving from what works to what might not work requires a big leap. One that most time-starved people will only make in extreme circumstances.

Innovation

Innovation is key to ambition. Ambitious organisations aim to set new standards in some or all aspects of their business model. This requires innovation. Innovative organisations understand that there is a cost to venturing into uncharted territory. That cost is failure. But even failure delivers value in the sense that it might highlight a misunderstanding of the problem being addressed. Or that the solution was lacking in some capacity. 'There is no failure, only feedback', is a presupposition associated with NLP (Neuro-Linguistic Programming), an approach geared towards personal self-development.

Unlike the industrial age, where there was sufficient certainty to create highly optimised business models, in the digital age the uncertainty is such that even the most successful business models are permanently 'in beta'. Beta being a term used in software development circles to refer to software that is almost, but not quite ready for release. It is likely that there are still a few bugs to be found.

This 'permanently in beta' mindset requires us to accept that we will never get to perfection. Our dominant position in the market will likely be transient at best, thus requiring continuous innovation to repeatedly wrestle back to a position of strength.

Innovation v invention

Not everyone is agreed on the definition of innovation, so I might simply be adding yet another definition. Innovation does not require the creation of something new. That is invention. Innovation can be thought of as an improvement of something that already exists, for example:

- A car that can double up as a drone in heavy traffic.
- The use of virtual assistants to offer 24-7 customer support.
- Reducing your price below your competitors' cost of production.

Some say that innovation is simply making a more useful version of something. In the corporate world, we talk a lot about innovation, primarily because it supports top line growth and cost reduction. Possibly, we talk less about invention because it does not convey the same degree of utility. Nonetheless organisations stockpile patents (ie inventions). In respect of pharmaceuticals those patents might well be very useful, lifesaving, in fact. My choice of the word innovation in the Biz 4.0 blueprint is more to be 'on trend'. Possibly I should call it I2 (Innovation and Invention). Let's just say that all inventions are innovations, but not all innovations are inventions.

T3

Innovation fuelled by the emergence of new technologies is something business leaders are encouraged to encourage. Too often in the past, we have seen the CIO approach the CEO/leadership team with ideas in respect of how emerging new technology trends, such as ecommerce, could revolutionise the market.

Often the leadership team lacked the vision to conceptualise the link to the business, and so dismissed the new technology as a '**toy**'.

Sometime later, it becomes apparent that the leadership teams of other players in the market were not so dismissive of the emerging technology. Customers like the ability to trade electronically. The technology has now become a '**threat**'.

Eventually every player in the market will incorporate this new technology into their business, and so it has become '**table stakes**'. Customers will no longer deal with vendors who have not embraced the new technology.

Digital leaders see every emerging technology as a potential market game changer. Even before they know what the change will look like.

The changing nature of risk

Shareholders vary in respect of their risk appetite. They don't explicitly pursue recklessness, but they see a link between risk and reward.

Traditionally from a leadership perspective, risk management meant the avoidance, elimination, or worst case, management of risk. But as we enter the digital age, the path to creating/acquiring value is to acquire risk.

Acquiring risk can take the form of:

- Acquiring a company, or even people.
- Investing in new products and services fuelled by emerging technologies.

Failure is a real possibility in such ventures. Digital leaders need to become comfortable with failure, and dare I say it, reward failure (as opposed to foolishness). If your organisation is built on a culture of spotless decision making, or with at least a belief that the path to success is one that avoids failure, then you are going to have to work hard to encourage entrepreneurial curiosity and experimentation.

We are naturally risk taking animals. However industrial era work has had a denaturing impact on our behaviour. For some, this will feel unsettling. They would rather the learned helplessness and mindlessness of following the operations manual, than the burden of unfettered opportunity and responsibility.

Incremental v radical

Innovation can be incremental or radical. Radical innovation might be considered as disruptive innovation. Applying collaborative consumption to the taxi industry would be regarded as a radical innovation in respect of business models. Using drones to airlift time-starved and affluent drivers out of traffic jams and onto their intended destination would be a radical use of new technology. Crowdsourced illness diagnosis, where not all the diagnoses are from doctors, is another example.

What constitutes radical innovation is a subjective matter. For many traditional organisations, radical innovations would be, well, too radical. The leadership team likely feel uncomfortable venturing into the unknown. It is unclear whether there would be a market waiting for such an innovation, and whether the market would be confused by this radical move. Incremental innovation is attractive because it doesn't require such a leap, and therefore exposes the organisation to less risk. Cars and computer processors come to mind.

Even Tesla cars are just an incremental innovation on modern day mainstream vehicles, even though they may seem functionally radical. In fact, radical innovation is a rarity. This is perhaps reflective of how denatured many of us have become, preferring to remain compliant and safe. It is likely that most organisations will take an incremental approach to innovation. It's less of a stretch for the leadership, the workers, and the market. So, will this consign established organisations to the slow lane in the digital age? There is no reason why conservative organisations cannot be successful taking an incremental innovation approach. They simply need to increase the velocity of their incremental innovation. Like compound interest, even small interest payments, if paid frequently enough, will deliver radical returns over time.

Having a culture that is innovation oriented, coupled with a set of processes that can smoothly convert ideas into value will be required. Keep in mind that if it wasn't for the innovative mindset of our ancestors, we would still be living in caves.

In fairness to the industrial era, it has been a period of great innovation. If you look around your home, you will see many innovative items that in some way or other makes your life easier, or gives you back the time you would have lost by having to take a more labour-intensive approach.

Frugal innovation

Silicon Valley is the spiritual home of high tech innovation. Organisations set up shop there in the hope that the spirit of Silicon Valley will rub off on their culture. Silicon Valley works, and it creates high value innovative organisations.

Silicon Valley is awash with venture capital. Burn rates and OPM (other people's money) litter the dialogue. If it doesn't work out, it's simply a case of convincing another gullible venture capitalist that they are about to be in at the start of a new Google.

But what of the innovations taking place in the backstreets of Calcutta, and other such places where there are no rivers of cash pouring into the region, where innovation is raw, and driven by need, as opposed to lifestyle enhancement?

Such places are the source of radical innovations such as the sub thousand-dollar car, or the fifty-dollar fridge. First world vendors might smirk at the quaintness of it all, believing that first world consumers would not be interested in such 'brand-questionable' offerings.

But we live in a world where many people were hit hard by the financial crash. The prospect of never owning their own home, or of having the same quality of life as their parents has led them to recalibrate their affluence aspirations.

Such people are embracing frugal capitalism, because they have no other choice. Such people will not only seek out such frugal innovations, but will become promoters of them. I anticipate that frugal innovation, particularly where there is a low impact on the Earth's resources, will threaten the established brands.

My message is that if you are planning to embrace innovation, you might consider extending your exploration beyond Silicon Valley.

Human considerations

- People have an ingrained need to be part of a tribe. Those organisations that build their organisations around that reality will attract and retain the best people. A worthy sense of purpose, and an innovative culture increasingly trumps a generous financial package and a questionable purpose.

- Your people might well be startled, as you migrate from an industrial business model. Ensure you explain the 'why' of this transition, what is in it for them, and how they in turn might transition in respect of their skills.

- Embracing the brain power of your people in respect of enterprise direction will be both empowering and threatening. Some will relish the opportunity. Others will seek a tribe that is not so demanding of them intellectually.

- Encourage your people to be themselves. The day of the perfect robo-professional is over. Plus, robots will soon do a better job in this respect. The less energy they must expend in suppressing their authentic selves, the more energy they will have for innovative delivery.

Capital considerations

- The tribe needs to keep one eye on the value it is creating, so the strategy needs to reflect this. The quality of your data capital will have a strong bearing on your strategic decision making, so developing it needs to be part of your strategy.

- Innovative cultures are more inclined to create intellectual capital, which in turn has a replenishing impact on your financial capital.

- Given that physical capital is not usually an active generator of value, I would encourage a strategy that aims to reduce ownership of physical assets. Tribes need somewhere to be based, but they do not want to be locked into a dwelling, particularly if the eating opportunities have moved elsewhere.

Take note

- We are designed for movement. People will be attracted to organisations that are also on the move, so to speak, particularly those following a path to a noble vision.

- Businesses are now primarily in the business of generating and pressure testing new business models. The advantages of any given business model in the digital age are likely to be transient at best.

- With the shifting power axis towards the talent and the blurring of the enterprise boundary, we are seeing the transformation of culture. This requires a more humble and empathetic leadership approach. Evolving the culture to one that embraces smart failure will not be a trivial exercise.

8 Attention

Overview

Paying attention is a survival skill. But we now live in a world where our attention has sufficient value to warrant it being sought. Every second you spend watching an amusing cat video is a second you have not spent on your own agenda, but that of the video poster. And possibly even that of the cat.

At the enterprise level, those organisations that pay the closest attention to the market will be in the best position to capitalise on emerging opportunities, and to respond appropriately to emerging threats. Given the changing nature of both opportunities and threats, having the ability to identify a related signal, and to quickly determine a suitable response, is key. New technologies are making this easier to do. And in many respects, your people are also market sensors. Their ability to sense, and to create, is strongly correlated to their available cognitive capacity. Thus, we need to build organisations that maximise this precious resource.

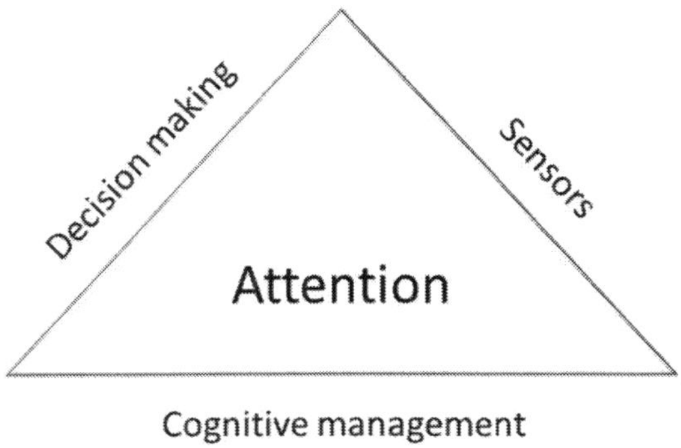

Figure 11 Attention

We are going to look at attention through the lenses of:

- Cognitive management.
- Sensors.
- Decision making.

Why is this important...

Distracted people with poor analytics capability, working on misleading/toxic data is guaranteed to send your organisation into a tailspin. Thus, attention management is a critical element of a digital age organisation.

Cognitive management

Cognitive leakage

The topic of cognitive management is not really understood by business leaders. If they did, they wouldn't force their people to grind their way through rush hour traffic/public transportation each day travelling to and from work.

I recently published a book, entitled Attention Dynamics, where I present several cognitive models that can be used to help people maximise their cognitive capacity. One of the models addresses the management of discretionary cognitive capacity. This is portion of our brain capacity that remains available when we factor in the chatter and disharmony that plagues our thinking. This discretionary cognitive capacity can be applied to creativity. Forcing your people to travel during the rush hour is a highly effective way of reducing their discretionary cognitive capacity. Your people might wake up creative on a Monday morning, but by Wednesday morning, they are waking up with the creative juices of a denatured cog worker.

Other ways to dissipate your people's cognitive capacity include:

- Micromanagement.
- Poor workplace design.
- Red tape.
- Poor IT systems.
- A toxic culture.
- Keeping people in the dark, eg. when rumours of a restructuring or a takeover are in circulation.

Attentive organisations strip away such cognitive sinks. Some organisations are so far advanced that they are focused on what has been referred to as marginal gains. What are the small improvements that can make a positive difference to cognitive availability.

Not all cognitive leakage is generated by the organisation. Unresolved relationship issues, poor health, and financial worries are just some of the other causes. Digital age talent engagement analytics will monitor all contributory factors that support the harvesting of their workers' cognitive capacity. This could be perceived as invasive, but it might equally be a win-win.

Cognitive enhancement

Removing cognitive leaks is only half the story. Creating the conditions for maximum cognitive engagement needs consideration. In essence, you need to build an environment that facilitates the workers' transition into a flow state. Flow is a psychological state where the worker is performing at full capacity, with a feeling of effortlessness. It's as if their body and mind have been commandeered by a higher force to produce great outputs. Top athletes, martial artists and authors are examples of professions that operate best in a state of flow.

The psychologist Mihaly Csikszentmihalyi produced the definitive coverage of this phenomenon in his aptly named book, entitled Flow. To tighten up my definition of flow, Csikszentmihalyi describes it as a mental and physical state in which we are performing at the top end of our skills capacity on tasks that stretch us to the full.

This rules out binge watching YouTube clips, even though you could argue that you are both fully and effortlessly engaged in the task. So, to achieve this desired flow state, you need to match the work to be done with the appropriate talent. If the work is under-stimulating, the person will become bored and disengaged. This could lead to poor quality work, and eventual loss of a very capable individual. You need to ensure that your corporate ambition is such that it will stretch great people. Otherwise you might as well lower your ambition, and brace yourself for the short trip to commercial oblivion.

From another perspective, you need to ensure that your 'soon to be great' people receive the learning and development investment required to raise their skills to a level whereby the work you need doing triggers a flow state.

Keep in mind:

- Great customers seek great work.
- Great work attracts great talent.
- Great talent attracts more great talent, and great customers.

Get this right and you will have created a 'perpetual motion' business. And in many respects, you will have created a 'perpetual emotion' business. One fuelled by turbo-charged grey matter. Keep in mind the opportunity to do great work comes from great ambition. Get that wrong, and you can replace the word 'great' with mediocre or poor in the above axioms. Digital leaders must 'go ambitious, or go home'. You can either engage the full cognitive capacity of great people, or you can partially engage the limited cognitive capacity of mediocre people.

This may sound elitist. Better to think of it as Darwinian. Keep in mind, we all have the same cognitive capacity, though the extent to which it is available for doing creative work varies from individual to individual. This top tier of talent is open to anyone who is willing to take ownership of their personal development, and cognitive management. This will not be easy for some people, given their personal circumstances, but it is possible.

I believe that it is the responsibility of both corporations and society to alert the cog workers as to what is happening in this respect, and to provide them with the tools to reinvent themselves for the digital age. It is only fair, plus it makes good economic sense.

The extent to which an organisation can harness human cognition will determine its success in the digital age. And again, fully engaged people, are highly attentive people. Highly attentive people can spot threats and opportunities before others. Highly attentive people have a deeper sense of what the market will value. As mentioned, increasingly workers will behave more like top athletes than compliant cogs. Such a shift raises the bar both in respect of their 'workplace' expectations, and the deliverables they are tasked to create.

The collective consciousness

I have mentioned the ability of robots to learn not just from their own experience, but from every other robot with which they are expected to collaborate. It is likely that we humans have a similar capacity, but it is too early in the evolution of neuroscience to discuss such a phenomenon in a mainstream business book. But I would encourage business leaders to create the conditions that would enable such a phenomenon to flourish.

Email is a mundane example of the necessary supportive infrastructure. Intranets are another example. Anything that supports co-working and sharing is to be encouraged. Much attention today is devoted to turning data into insight. The next steps are in turning insight into knowledge, and knowledge into wisdom. Technologies that support this are to be encouraged. Could your workplace be reengineered to facilitate knowledge sharing? Again, this is not an exhortation to go open plan everywhere. But there is much that can be done to engineer the social dynamics of your organisation.

Could you put in place metrics that encourage collaborative behaviour? Imagine a world where sales staff do not get paid a commission on business they land, but on the business they help others to land.

Building sociality into your key performance indicators meets an important anthropological driver. It binds your people, if only for the duration of a project, and acts as a cognitive stimulant.

Sensors

IoT

It is through our own in-built sensors that we see and engage with the world. We are only conscious of a small fraction of all the data that passes through our organic sensors. To be aware of everything would be too much for our brain to handle, and runs the risk that important data, such as a growl, would be overlooked. Thus, our mental faculties provide data filtering functionality. This enables us to spend less time thinking and more time moving/doing.

The downside of data filtering is that what we imagine is happening beyond us is simply a perception of reality, rather than reality. More often than not, it is a good approximation. But when coloured with biases, and emotions, it can become a pretty distorted picture. This in turn can lead to inappropriate responses on our part.

Corporations need to build a picture of the environment in which they exist. Again, there is a danger of data overload. So, choosing what data to capture is a critical aspect of your business model. We will come back to this.

The arrival of the so-called internet of things (IoT) is set to revolutionise the extent to which we can sense our environment. Organisations that produce fitness trackers will have intimate knowledge about their customers. Organisations that provide aircraft components will be best placed to anticipate, and pre-empt, aviation disasters. Think of the objects that form part of your environment/market. Objects that might be considered dumb, ie. they have no intelligence built into them.

Such objects might include:

- Trolleys.
- Overalls.
- Bricks.
- Tablets.
- Flower pots.
- Staplers.
- Staples.

If retailers added sensor technology to their supermarket trolleys, they could:

- Identify who their best customers are, and redirect them to the express checkout, rather than limit that privilege to their low spending ('5 items or less') customers.
- Make recommendations based on the items gathered as to how they could be used. And how they could be used with other, as yet unretrieved items, to create new and interesting meals.
- Direct customers to where they can find the additional items.
- Trigger shelf replenishment, and real-time shelf configuration.

I encourage you to take an inventory of your dumb, or so called 'dark assets', and brainstorm how they might be 'smartened up' for value creation purposes.

Implementing IoT

It is very early days in respect of IoT adoption. There are plenty of issues to be resolved, including IT architecture, security, and communication protocols.

The concept of edge processing is taking shape. More and more of the data processing will take place in situ. This requires a highly-decentralised IT architecture. Unfortunately, each sensor also provides a gateway for hackers to enter the organisation. Trusting the data that your dark assets discharge will be a major challenge.

Such issues might be resolved by cooperation within given sectors. Or that is how they might have been resolved in the industrial era. The sector boundaries are blurring, so again this is likely to be a battle of the ecosystems. And it won't necessarily be the big established players who take the lead.

There is no reason why the likes of Intel or Apple can't come to dominate the automotive industry. They are unlikely to get into the business of producing cars. But the increasing functionality/value that cars will provide, beyond transportation, will likely be processor/app/data driven.

Some of us might be concerned that Amazon has recorded every keystroke we have ever made on their websites. But with smart virtual assistants, such as Amazon Echo, every conversation you and your family have in the privacy of your own home is now part of Amazon's data pool. I suspect younger people will perceive this as a valuable capability. The more Amazon knows me, the better their recommendations will be. For them, this is the modern-day equivalent of having a butler, without the passive aggressive judgemental sneering.

Human sensors

Imagine recruiting people based on their market sensitivity. General knowledge of the terrain in which your organisation operates is valuable. Having real-time sensitivity to market fluctuations is more so.

This finger on the market pulse capability is to be found in people who are well connected and socially active. Invariably they will read and discuss market news, and in the process, develop their own intuitive sense of how the near future might play out. I find such discussions valuable in both honing and reconstructing my perspectives.

And as mentioned, to an increasingly large extent, the social networks of your people will become an extension of the enterprise's brain trust. Each individual in each personal network is playing a part in building the market sensitivity of your people, and thus your organisation. Of course, your clients and suppliers are also valuable nodes in this informal intelligence network.

It is potentially risky to make important business decisions off the back of what might be patchy intelligence. One would hope that the bigger the brain trust, the better the perspectives. At least the individual interpretations, biases and agendas would be smoothed out by having access to a larger array of 'human sensors'. I would be inclined to use your human sensors as the basis for a hypothesis, which you can then test using a more quantitative approach.

Using your people in this informal intelligence crowdsourcing manner will be somewhat unsettling for the market analyst organisations who traditionally charge high fees to tell you what is happening outside your front door.

Those organisations with the best sensors will have the best perception of what is happening in their market, particularly those who can build a consolidated picture based on integrating the inputs from their technology and human sensors. If your approach to attentiveness is anything less than a NASA mission control centre, you will be perceived as a reckless leader presiding over a neurologically inert organisation.

Chief Listening Officer

With this in mind, you might consider appointing a Chief Listening Officer. It would be their responsibility to monitor the market. Imagine a NASA mission control centre with large screens displaying data from sources, including:

- IoT devices deployed within your organisation.
- IoT devices deployed in the market.
    - Embedded in your products.
- Human sensors.
- Social media feeds.
- Third party intelligence feeds.
    - 'Paid for' and publicly available.

These would be fed into a data repository, that includes tools to automatically 'clean' and classify the inputs, as well as analytic tools to interpret the consolidated data.

On these screens are displayed various colour coded metrics to flag whether all is good (green), or attention is advised (orange), or attention is urgently needed (red).

This is of course what digital leaders require, but accessible via a mobile device. And of course, these metrics should be available to all your people. Everybody should be prepared to change modes, when the "Houston, we have a problem" alert is risen. The extent to which this doesn't sound like your current operating model is a measure of the transformation journey you have in front of you. Your organisation cannot afford to be anything less than in real-time contact with your market. Inward looking, terrain-indifferent tribes don't exist today for very good reason. Modern organisations are no different.

Decision making

Knowing that a bear is outside the tent is useful intelligence. But it is the decisions you make based on that reality that will determine whether you will emerge from the encounter unscathed. Digital organisations are designed to be attentive, and to act on what they observe and uncover.

Analytics

Analytics is not a new concept. The need to present data and information in a meaningful manner precedes the industrial era. The emergence of database technologies in the last century provided the fertile conditions to grow the analytics capability that is available today.

As both a participant and an observer of the IT market, it was interesting to watch the analytics products market grow steadily regardless of the prevailing economic conditions as we changed millennia.

People and organisations need to make decisions, and increasingly those decisions were data-driven. The established IT providers saw the value-add in analytics, and consequently all the original mainstream analytics (aka as business intelligence) players have been acquired.

Analytics has evolved significantly. Today the analytics tools are graphically-rich, thus making the data-driven insights easier to consume.

The tools today harness AI, and can operate in real-time. Thus, social media feeds can be panned for insight. Sentiment analysis comes to mind. The shift from market darling to toxic pariah is all too easy given the group think/witch-hunt mentality that social media encourages. The data associated with this behaviour can be harnessed to predict, for example, the likely direction a share price might take. Predictive analytics is increasingly an essential weapon in the digital leader's armoury. Successfully anticipating demand will lead to better supply chain management. Analytics tools are steadily improving in respect of management of risk and the detection of fraud.

The challenge for digital organisations is to ensure their analytics capability feeds from a coherent array of data sets. IT was simpler when all the organisation's data was neatly structured in a relational database. Such databases still exist, but the data formats have extended beyond date, numbers and characters. Images, sound and video are now part of the mix. Making these analytics-ready requires investment.

Not all data is real-time. Some sources may be sporadic. Others may be delivered end of day, or end of week. Piecing these together to form a coherent perspective of reality requires investment. Deciding what not to capture is equally important.

Increasingly data has a geospatial significance, and so is better shown in that context. If you sell home insurance, it is informative to understand where your best customers live. One approach is to receive a tabulated report, perhaps ordered by post or zip code. A better approach would be to plot their location onto a map. And to then overlay that map with household crime data and/or property valuation data. Augmented analytics will increasingly contribute to the richness of the decision-making tools.

Facility managers could study the repair work carried out in a building over a set period. The location of the repairs might well be symptomatic of something structural, which would not have been picked up if the repairs where simply listed in a report.

Traditionally analytics tools were user-driven; the user decides what they want to analyse. Thanks to developments in machine learning (a branch of AI), the analytics tools can suggest where your attention might be best placed. Machine learning is getting increasingly better at identifying patterns and weak signals that might be indicative of a threat, trend or opportunity. Humans are limited when it comes to detecting patterns in large and disparate data sets. AI addresses this human frailty.

Digital business leaders are adept at harnessing the power of analytics tools. As we will see, they recognise that tools should not be constrained to boardroom users.

Decentralised leadership

I have made several references to decentralised leadership. The impact of a given action is reduced significantly for each decision-making gate it must pass through before it is approved. At the very least, it leads to arthritic action in the face of opportunity or threat.

In nature, extinction is a real issue. Most species that have ever existed are now extinct. As species go, humans might be considered as arrivistes in respect of the length of our existence. If we look at some of the more established species, we will notice that many of them have a leaderless/decentralised leadership/shared leadership approach.

Birds take turns to lead the flock, not because they are leadership material, but because of the inherent dynamics of the group. Ants do not have leaders, yet seem to get things done. Trees, bacteria and viruses similarly do not have a command structure. Terrorists, with their cellular organisational structure, often outflank better equipped traditional military because they can make decisions at the cellular level. The special forces units of the armed forces have learned to similarly operate in this decentralised manner.

Seeking permission is an improvisation dampener. In the fog of war, being unable to improvise puts you at a severe disadvantage.

It may take a while before nature's highly visible leadership lessons are acknowledged and acted upon. But nobody would argue that there is a need to decentralise leadership, such that those in the field can act swiftly in the face of an opportunity or an incident.

This sounds great in principle, but the potential risks can make it unappealing for leaders to release their grip. Though this should only be a concern if you fear that the decision-making capability of those in the field is inferior to yours. The reality is that they are closer to the action, and have a better understanding of the associated circumstances. In any case, this is an opportunity to use analytics technologies to assist the field operatives in their decision making. It would be a mistake to give a new entrant banking clerk free rein in respect of their mortgage granting capability. Analytics tools can be used to make the decision using data in respect of the prospective mortgagee. Thus, in this case the decision-making rules are institutionalised and woven into the business process logic.

The more decisions you can delegate, the less decisions you need to make. The fewer decisions you need to make, the more of your cognitive capacity will be available for strategic and innovative matters.

Heart and gut

In the last decade or so there has been some talk about how leaders who simply rely on their head for decision making are to some extent incomplete.

Our nervous system is not centralised around our cranium, but has similar neural concentrations in our heart and in our guts. In other words, we have three brains. It is said that our brain brain is the source of our creativity. Our heart brain is our source of compassion. And our gut (or enteric) brain is our source of courage. Utilising our three brains is no doubt likely to result in better decisions. Courageous, compassionate and creative leaders are essential in the digital age. And so are courageous, compassionate and creative people.

But in this volatile world, it is too risky to set a course based on one, or a handful of individuals. We need to harness the brains of all our people. But even more importantly in the digital age, decisions need to be supported by genuine data.

Augmented intelligence

I have covered this already, but raise it again because in respect of decision making there is still quite a journey ahead. Holographic and virtual reality technologies will eventually be woven into our decision-making tools.

Biological stimulants may well be as freely available as coffee. Virtual assistants with access to the world's largest supercomputers via the cloud will support our decision making.

We have come a long way already. Many of us hold the world's knowledge in our pocket, thanks to our internet-ready phone. But there is the tedious matter of extracting it from one's pocket. Wearable technology, such as wrist bands and glasses, will eliminate this inconvenience. Imagine whilst interviewing a candidate employee, you are reviewing their LinkedIn profile, ten most recent Amazon purchases, and their top one hundred web destinations using the head-up display capability of your smart glasses. Or via your recently installed smart eyeball. Those organisations that can make the best decisions will win. What this means biologically and technologically in the years to come is anybody's guess. But whatever path this takes, you would be advised to monitor it closely.

Boardroom as an algorithm

So where are we heading with decision making? If we zoom a few years into the future, it is likely that the Fortune 500 will comprise companies where each 'boardroom' is on a rack in a datacentre. In other words, human leaders will be redundant, and each organisation will be run by an AI-driven algorithm. The possibility that Fortune magazine might get into the data centre business to house these prestigious companies cannot be ruled out.

This is not so far-fetched. There have already been robot appointments to the board. And the World Economic Forum sees this trend kicking in around 2025. You may well be considering your career trajectory in the light of this. Automation is no respecter of seniority.

I mention this, not so much as to warn you of your impending professional demise, but to highlight that we all need to transform at a pace that is slightly faster than the evolution of new technology. Think of there being three horizons to consider:

1. The transition to a human-fuelled organisation.
2. The transition to an augmented human organisation.
    a. Intimate integration of human and technology capability.
3. The transition to a human-free organisation.

This book is preparing you for the journey to the first horizon. The second horizon will take us into the world of genomics, nootropics and neuro-technology integration. In my view, it is the role of today's business leaders to transition their organisations through these end game steps. But of course, there are many variables that might well delay these horizons, such that they never come to pass. My enteric (gut) feeling suggests otherwise, but again this is just an opinion, and not a fact.

It is worth being aware that AI works well at drawing inferences from large datasets. It is not so good where the data is sparse. Humans on the other hand, thanks to millions of years of evolutionary programming, are very impressive when it comes to making decisions with very small datasets. Possibly there will still be a role for human leaders in ultra-niched boutique organisations, where the markets are so small that AI-driven decision making would be disastrous / unavailable.

But we must keep in mind that strategic decision making is no longer a burden to be carried solely by the c-suite team. We are moving towards a business model that harnesses the decision-making power of all the talent. The role of the modern leader is not so much to make the big decisions, but to put an associated framework in place to devolve both the operational and strategic decision-making processes.

Ultimately, extreme decentralisation of decision-making leads again to a leaderless organisation. We will need leaders to handle this transformation. Once complete, leaders will need to reskill with a view to re-entering the market as a talented 'gun for hire'. Perhaps the smart move today, would be to imagine this future scenario, and start your own personal transformation in parallel with the organisational journey you are presiding over.

Human considerations

- It is in our nature to pay attention. You can be sure your ancestors paid attention. If they hadn't, you wouldn't be here today. Organisations cannot afford to hermetically seal themselves from the market. Market sensitivity is critical. Given that talent is key to your success, paying attention to the engagement levels of your people will be similarly critical.

- Anthropologically, we are blessed with sensors. Our senses enable us to be curious, and to be cautious. Attentive organisations recognise this aspect of our nature, and so do not deny us the opportunity to be both curious, and to have some degree of autonomy.

- Building an attentive tribe, and equipping them with the best analytics tools, is a primary objective for digital leaders.

Capital considerations

- Your data capital is going to play a major role in your organisation's attentiveness. You are encouraged to invest in your data capital. This will pay for itself many times over as the quality of your organisation's decisions improve accordingly.

- Given the frailty of corporate brands in the digital age, and thus in turn your brand capital, paying attention to market sentiment will enable you to act fast if your reputation takes a downhill trajectory.

- Paying attention to the engagement levels of your people will enable you to address problems before they cascade into a mass talent exodus. This is critical to maintaining your growth in respect of human capital.

Take note

- An attentive organisation feels more like a high-octane cognitive gym, rather than resignation-fuelled labour camp. Or more specifically a high-octane hybrid mission control centre/gym. Like a war room, to introduce yet another analogy, everyone is switched on to what is happening and prepared to change direction based on reality. Everything is happening in real time.
    - I have seen sleepy, family owned, Swiss private banks transform into Madison Avenue creative agencies as a consequence of their digital transformation. Once you decide to truly engage with the real world, you need to keep up, or perish.

- The currency of human capital is cognitive capacity. Digital age organisations do not squander this precious resource through poor management, bureaucracy or confrontational IT systems. In fact, they boost it by having their people perform at their highest capacity in handling the most stimulating of challenges.

- Attentive organisations do not cut corners or costs when it comes to analytics. A martial artist can have the greatest skills in the world, but if she is blindfolded then she will struggle to apply them effectively. I appreciate that Luke Skywalker is an exception in this respect.

- 'Rubbish in rubbish out' applies to analytics. Top of the range analytics tools will serve up misleading insights if they are feeding from a poor data model. Digital age organisations architect their data model to ensure the incoming data from the various sources are weaved together to accurately reflect reality.

- To produce a data model that accurately reflects reality you will need to have a data gathering strategy that encompasses humans, technology, social media, publicly available data sources, and feeds from third parties.

- Attentiveness is the secret to success, whether it is a tribe or a modern corporation made up of digital hunter gatherers.

9 Adaptability

Overview

Adaptability is a prerequisite for all living things. Tribes that failed to adapt to the ice age, came to a brutal end. Tribes that adapted to the agricultural revolution capitalised on developing trading relationships with the agriculturists.

Adaptability has always been a requirement for businesses. The arrival of the car was an adaptation to our increasing need to travel distances that made walking unattractive. But it is more important today than ever because the clock speed of the market appears to be steadily increasing. In the past, one could predict market dominance in a year's time with some accuracy given the glacial speed at which the market operated. That is no longer the case. Those enjoying dominance today need to operate with the zeal of a young challenger and with the urgency associated with finding yourself on a burning platform.

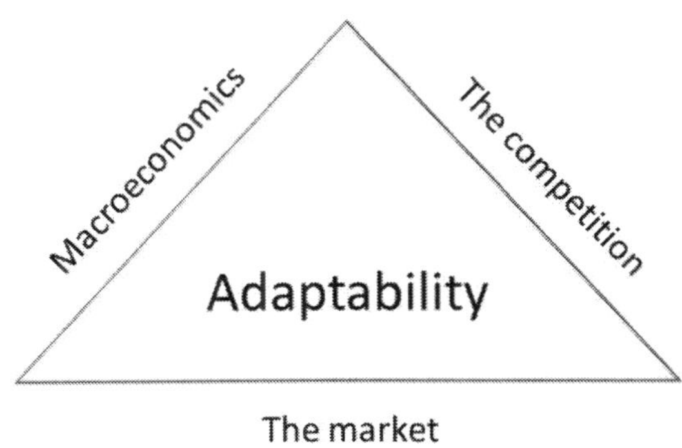

Figure 12 Adaptability

In this chapter, we are going to explore adaptability through the lenses of:

- Macroeconomics.
- The market.
- The competition.

Why is this important…

Adapt or die is the premise that underpins evolutionary theory. It equally applies to organisations in the digital age, though the rate of adaptation required is unprecedented. Organisations that do not have adaptability built into the business will find the digital age to be very stressful. The good news is that whether you act on this or not, the period of stress will be relatively short lived.

Macroeconomics

Tribes are very conscious of their environment. It provides valuable information that will determine the tribe's subsequent actions. Being uninterested or unable to interpret the environment makes the tribe vulnerable. Similarly, it is a business leader's responsibility to keep on top of the wider factors that might impact the organisation's journey towards its vison. Let us look at some of the key factors that are likely to have a bearing on your business.

Globalisation

Globalisation is not a new phenomenon. In fact, international trading dates back many millennia. Large scale globalisation emerged in the early nineteenth century. Today everything seems to be connected to everything thanks to new technology and the supply chain tails of the world's largest companies.

However, international trade and cross border finance have flattened, which might imply that we have hit 'peak globalisation'. But this is not the case. It is simply that globalisation in the digital age needs to be studied in terms of data flows and not 'stuff', according to the McKinsey Global Institute. The economic impact of 'data goods' has now exceeded that of physical goods. Surely this is a sign that the digital age has commenced.

Adaptable organisations are going to be those that can migrate their offerings to reflect this growth in digital opportunity.

Emerging middleclass

The industrial revolution created a substantial middleclass in the US and Western Europe. Japan benefited from the second wave of growth, just after the second world war. Today, according to professional services provider EY, Asia alone has more middleclass people than the entire population of the European Union. This is expected to expand by three billion in the next few decades as the emerging economies 'join the club'.

This will have a substantial bearing on where the business action will take place. Will the first world countries become mere supply chain nodes for the emerging countries?

In any case, the prospect of 3 billion new customers is not to be sniffed at.

Talent

By talent, I don't mean people, or even 'can do' millennials. I am referring to people who can do things that technology cannot do that has economic value. That is a small subset of the people working today. Whilst automation is destroying jobs in large numbers, there is, as laboured in this book, a growing need for creative workers. The war for talent is getting increasingly violent. You are encouraged to make talent management your number one priority.

Technology

None of us are blind to the role information technology is playing in respect of changing the nature of everything. We are living in exponential times, thus making it difficult to anticipate what business will look like in just a few years from now. I have mentioned the impact that robots and AI will have. And who knows how this will play out as the AI-fuelled robots take over the process of technology innovation.

But in my view, even this will appear mundane compared to the advances we will witness in the biosciences. In many respects, the twentieth century was the information age. The twenty first century is likely to be the biological age. Augmented humanity is slowly becoming mainstream. This will have a profound impact on society. And of course, it will have a profound impact on the services your organisation offer, and the way you engage with your people.

Regulation

Some readers will cringe at my freewheeling, maverick suggestions on how businesses need to be structured for the digital age. They would suggest that I have never had exposure to a regulated industry. For the record, I have. Regulation is a reality in some industries, and corporate governance is a reality for all business leaders. Trying to develop innovative services, in an ever-accelerating world, whilst your wrists are tied up with red tape, is not sustainable.

Fortunately, some regulators are realising this. Recently, I chaired an event at Sibos, an annual, global financial services gathering, and had several banking regulators involved on stage. It was refreshing to hear them talk of using a 'controlled' Minimum Viable Product (MVP) model in respect of introducing new regulation. Perhaps it is a sign of the digital age, when we have regulators behaving like Silicon Valley start-ups.

Digital transformation work I am doing in the professional services sector has led me to believe that the regulator should be regarded as a business partner, rather than a business thwarter.

As attitudes to risk evolve, there will be a need to adjust regulations and best governance practice to reflect this new reality.

War/Terrorism

War and terrorism impact each of us every day. Your country may not be at war, but what with globalisation, your organisation is likely to be feeling the consequences of war elsewhere. If your country or company is the target of religious or ideological extremism, the anticipation of attack is sufficient to distract the leadership from their primary activities. Today, if you have something, or produce something, of value, you must operate on the basis that you are under constant siege in respect of cyber attackers. Your enemy can be anything from a bored teenager through to a state sponsored cyber militia. Today war and terrorism, from a business perspective, can be considered a tax on creating value. The extent to which you pay will be determined in part by what you stand for, and in part because you just happen to represent, in some way or other, the interests of the opposing side.

FX

Foreign exchange rates play a significant role in the fortunes of international organisations. Fluctuations can be good for exports or good for imports. If your offerings rely on a supply chain that operates in another currency, then you are at the mercy of the associated exchange rate. Exchange rate manipulation appears to be a weapon used alongside cyber attacks to wage war on an enemy without firing a bullet. The choice of markets your organisation operates in and your choice of international suppliers need to be considered within the context of a holistic currency management framework. When operating in an international arena, just because we have great offerings and a great demand does not mean that our success is assured.

But in fairness, it can work the other way, whereby 'so so' offerings with some demand might yield great profits because of favourable exchange rates. Though I would not build a business model that is reliant on this outcome.

Demographics

Demographics is an important consideration in respect of your market, and your own people. This becomes more pointed in the digital age.

- Creating a funky user interface might backfire, if the target users are over forty, and the text size you have used presumes the visual acuity of a nineteen-year-old.
- Similarly using mainstream social media to capture the attention of early adopters who only hangout on niche platforms.
- Gamifying the workplace might be a natural extension of home life (at least the video games aspect of it), but may alienate older workers.
- Personalisation is great for some, and creepy for others, so where do you draw the line?

Factoring in demographics get more complicated in the digital age as more communication channels appear, coupled with an emerging omni-channel approach to engaging with people. The friend-lification of channels, whereby, for example, the help desk operator, on seeing your customer record, asks, "Is it okay if I call you Ade?". Senior citizens, with more time on their hands, may well appreciate a seemingly personalised transaction. Others, more time-starved, would prefer a virtual assistant that keeps the small talk to a minimum.

The demographic profile of your target markets and your choice of business locations, will drive the way you engage with customers and talent. Today accurate demographic data is difficult to come by in respect of the emerging economies. As they become important both as a source of talent and as a market of affluent consumers, those with the best demographic information will be at a considerable advantage.

Natural

Natural disasters have the power to disrupt supply chains and 'turn off' markets. This reality needs to be factored into your organisation's risk management process.

There is a sense that natural disasters are on the increase. Possibly it's just the case that such disasters are better reported. More likely it is the case that not all of these natural disasters are truly natural and are most likely anthropogenic in nature.

Human-induced climate change is likely responsibly for tropical cyclones and forest fires. Both customers and prospective candidates will take an increasingly dim view if they feel that your brand is a contributor.

Then there is the matter of natural resources. Electronic equipment appears to require a myriad of constituents, including many rare-earth elements. According to the human rights organisation, Amnesty International, the cobalt needed for your phone may have been acquired using child labour. Organisations that inadvertently, or otherwise, encourage such unacceptable behaviour will face a backlash from the market. Though possibly consumers will delay their outrage until a provider steps forward with a 'clean' supply chain option.

The need for rare elements will likely be one of the major drivers in respect of mining missions to other planets.

The market

A key aspect of being adaptable is in understanding the market. The quicker you can detect market changes, and respond accordingly, the more likely you will thrive.

Extending the tribe

If we think of your organisation as a tribe, then we can either think of your target market as a collection of other tribes, or an extension of your own.

Here's a way of deciding which model is best for you.

Supplier – Where you provide services to other parties, with minimised risk to either party, you can consider your targets as tribes. They can drop you when it suits them. Most likely because they can find better value elsewhere. Similarly, you can drop them if the relationship gets too onerous, as they are just one of many.

Partner – Where you provide services to another party, and there is a shared degree of risk. You have the potential to both win big, so such targets can be considered an extension of your tribe. As you both have 'skin in the game', there is the risk of loss too. You are unlikely to drop each other, because to some extent at least, you have entwined your destinies.

Partnerships are like marriage in that they are a big commitment. Many providers talk about partnerships, but are too set in their ways, and so will be 'out the door' with their suitcase, at the first sign of discord.

Many organisations do not even think of their customers as separate tribes. 'Prey' would be a more accurate term. From a buyer's perspective, if the supplier is hassling you to close the deal in the run up to the end of their financial quarter, you can be sure that marriage isn't on the cards.

The partner model is not just some high-end Business to Business (B2B) concept. It is applicable to high volume transactional Business to Consumer models (B2C) too. Working with the market to develop the next wave of services is a form of partnership, as are loyalty programmes.

The value proposition

What your organisation does for its customers and how the service will be consumed needs to be clear. This is all part of the Ambition success factor activity. Perhaps you will structure your offering so that it is given away for free because the revenue will emerge from advertising. Or possibly you will take a freemium (a subset of the services is available for free), or position it as a high value, high margin offering.

Often, particularly amongst the technology vendors, I see the sales guys march into the meeting with a high value proposition (in their minds at least), and walk out with the task to negotiate a deep discount with their manager on behalf of the buyer. What went wrong?

There is at least a generation or two of sellers who do not really understand what constitutes value in the eyes of senior (CxO level) buyers. They stick to product features, or fail to convince the buyer that, whilst they don't see it in their market today, there is a digital tsunami on its way.

Often such sellers are transaction rather than relationship oriented. They do not see the need to establish trust and relevance, so they just dive straight into the sales pitch.

Loyalty, fickleness and habit

If you own a bar in the tourist section of town, it makes no sense to try to sign customers up to your loyalty programme, particularly when the bar is three deep in plaid, baseball caps and lanyarded cameras. Why bother? You are unlikely to see them again. Where there is the potential to engage with the customer on a regular basis, it might well be worth getting them 'onto the programme'. With this in mind, global hotel chains often try to catch weary business travellers, at their most vulnerable.

In the digital age, it is likely that we are all so distracted, and dealing with so many providers that we cannot conceptually cope with belonging to yet another loyalty programme. Given this, it would be much more convenient all around, if instead of trying to pin down the client with a pitch to their consciousness. You secure them by pitching to their subconsciousness, by exploiting their habitual behaviour. Turning your service into a habit is the new sales model for the digital age.

If you add to this the fact that your service is likely to evolve into an online utility offering, you need to be thinking about SaaS (Service as a Service). With such a model, if the habit isn't established quickly, you will have a cashflow problem.

Service is the new sales

There is a natural relationship between cost, risk and value. For the typical sales professional selling 'hit and run' offerings, the major risk to them is that the sale will fall through. Implementation risks are someone else's problem.

But we are entering a world where the customer wants higher value from the organisation, and they don't want the sales process to be decoupled from the delivery service.

For me, this is indicative of service becoming the new sales. Service professionals who typically spend most of their time on the clients' sites are in a very strong position to talk with the buyers, and highlight new buying opportunities, without coming across as salesy. They can engage in deeper conversations than the typical sales person, because that is the nature of their job.

In my view, smart organisations will explore extending the skillset of their service function, rather than automating it. Sales professionals need to reflect as to how they stay in play with such an evolving dynamic.

Relational capital

This is an important element of human capital. What your people know about your clients and prospects is of value. Generally speaking, business development professionals are unlikely to share what they know, unless they are incentivised to do so.

Institutionalising relationship knowledge is a challenge for most organisations. If I have worked hard to develop a deep relationship with a commercially-significant CEO, I am not going to add all I know about them to an enterprise customer relationship management database, so that others can use my hard-earned intelligence to cash in. In any case, the CEO would find it strange if they received a call from one of your new-entrant business developers enquiring about the wellness of the family's pet tortoise.

Keeping track of what your 'targets' have bought, or are likely to buy is one thing. Keeping track of the depth of the relationship is another, and one that is more important. A large database of customers might at first seem impressive, until it is discovered that they have only ever bought once. Having some sort of scoring system that extends from, say, 'hostile' to 'personal' in terms of relationship depth can be used to assess individual relationships. And by collating the scores, it can be used to understand relational health at an organisational level.

Deeper relationships are not obtained by making every communication the carrier of some form of sales payload. Social media endeavours that are really commercial Trojan horses are increasingly brand damaging. In the digital age, it is necessary to give in order to get. This is rewarding in its own right. Smart leaders build strong client relationships by looking for ways to be of genuine help, regardless of whether the outcome has a commercial benefit. Some companies will abuse this generosity. Many will appreciate it.

Lever the community

What I have just described is perhaps more relevant to the B2B marketplace. Though even B2C customers want to feel respected, so you are encouraged to explore how you can add value at scale to a large consumer base. Web-based relationships make this possible. If you have a sufficiently large customer base, you might consider seeking out services your community would value, and on their behalf negotiating a group discount. This could cover anything from discounted travel to reduced home insurance. One of the benefits of creating an ecosystem is that if you can scale it up sufficiently, the service providers have no choice but to comply with whatever conditions you choose.

Habits

Returning to the topic of habits. When I talk about relational capital, there is a sense that the aim is to build an array of warm human connections, like an extended (idealised) family. The reality is that in this age of distraction, many clients will not be looking for a relationship, because they already have too many.

Thus, the variant on this relationship game is to neurologically reprogramme your market. Mercifully, this does not require invasive surgery. As already mentioned, your organisation's ability to ingrain habits into its market is what is needed. I use Amazon, not necessarily because I am an Amazon fan, but because they have my credit card details, and the process is so slick that I do it without even thinking of alternative approaches. So, what can you do to habituate the behaviours of your target market? If they start salivating when you ring a bell, then you have this approach mastered.

Creating an ecosystem

Only the very brave, or rich, would try to wrestle away the clients of ecosystem owners such as Facebook, Google, Amazon or Apple. They are extremely well established, and in the main, they didn't have to build their ecosystem by dragging individuals away, one by one, from an existing platform. So, if your market has an established player, your options are to:

- Find another market.
- Develop a niche ecosystem for a subset of the target market.

Keep in mind that building an ecosystem can be useful for binding your customer base together. You do not necessarily need to make it a cash generating platform. Perhaps your organisation specialises in sports equipment for middle aged people who have just come out of a divorce and are looking to 'buff themselves up' for market re-entry. The provision of online dating functionality would better align your brand with the actual benefits your market is seeking.

The competition

Competition inevitably emerges when two or more parties seek a resource that cannot be shared. It is a reality of nature and of business. That stated, it is possible that multiple providers might be in a situation where they can access the same resource (customer pool).

Multiple taxi firms operating from one railway station comes to mind. One firm could decide that if it acquired or eliminated the others, it would create a sufficient supply-demand imbalance to significantly ramp up its profits. If successful, it would have a monopoly, and invariably the market would suffer for it. Customer dissatisfaction would pave the way for a cheaper new-entrant player to enter the market, and competition, along with downward price pressure would resume. But then Uber arrives, reinventing the game, with its own set of rules.

If you are not the Uber of your industry, or its equivalent has not yet arrived in your industry, you had best prepare for them. In the digital age, as we have seen, it is a case of disrupt or be disrupted.

Being adaptable means being able to operate successfully on a battlefield where the enemy is unrecognisable, until they draw their sword.

The Art of War

Wars are to be avoided. In the animal kingdom, aggression is ritualised, so that disputes can be settled without blood being shed. Picture two male lions taking it in turn to display their break dancing prowess, in order to settle a mating dispute.

But sometimes the enemy/competition must be banjaxed for good. And if you operate in a competitive market, it is likely that you have enemies. Military strategy has had many millennia to evolve. The fifth century BC treatise, entitled the Art of War, contains advice that is very relevant to the digital age, including:

- Do not engage until you have created the conditions for certain victory.
- Destroying your enemy's will to fight is preferable to physically conquering them.
- Know when to attack and when to flee.
- Avoid prolonged warfare.

- Do not repeat previously successful tactics, rather be adaptable to the myriad of circumstances that present themselves in each situation.

As mentioned, strategy in the digital age is not dissimilar to military strategy. The ability to lead in a chaotic environment, where you do not have a full understanding of the situation, and are repeatedly suffering unforeseen losses, will be the marque of a true digital leader.

Digital aggressiveness

Here is an extract from one of the posts from my **Digital Strategy blog**, which will help you reflect on whether your organisation is battle-ready:

** start of post extract ** Here is a mechanism for measuring your disruption readiness/digital aggression. There are nine levels. Here they are in ascending order of aggressiveness:

1. **Asleep**: Your organisation is oblivious to what is happening in the market. You are unlikely to have invested in analytics technologies. It is likely that your business is so good that your sales staff can merrily take the orders from the comfort of their hermetically-sealed office.
2. **Distracted:** You have the analytics tools, and maybe have even invested in the Internet of Things (IoT)/sensor technologies. However, your leadership is too focused on internal matters. Or worse still, it is overly paying attention to the strategic plan. Yes. Strategic planning in the traditional industrial-era sense is now considered a new genre of fiction.
3. **Yoga:** At this stage, you are very tuned to the market. Your organisation is mindful of the threats and opportunities. As well as having great **attention skills**, it is impressively agile. Unfortunately, the market clock speed has accelerated somewhat from the good old industrial days. Agility and attentiveness are of no use if you do not have the speed of response.

4 **Parkour:** This is also known as free running. Exponents have all the traits needed to survive on the Savanna or in the urban jungle. If disruption looms, they can retreat at speed, no matter what the terrain. They can even approach the threat at speed with the view to hopping over them, so that they are unable to engage. This might be considered a digitally-defensive posture.

5 **Aikido:** This is a martial art that uses the energy of the opponent to 'restore harmony', should they launch an attack. It might be considered 'yoga at speed'. Practitioners can deal with attacks, but philosophically cannot bring themselves to inflict pain on the attacker. So once restrained, the attacker is released. Of course, they may attack again. But the aikido practitioner will happily repeat the process until the attacker, in a bewildered state, simply walks off. Again, this is a digitally-defensive posture.

6 **Striking martial arts:** Aikido has no strikes, so it is very difficult to get a fight going on a Saturday night in town; aikido practitioners would have it no other way. But there are several martial arts that are resplendent in their striking armoury. Think Karate, Jiu Jitsu, Boxing and Muay Thai as examples. In broader terms, think mixed martial arts. As a casual brawler, you don't really want to mess with these guys. They are both defensive and offensive artists. That said, unfortunately, on the street, there is typically no allowance given by the attacker in respect of the need to warm up first. And similarly, the attacker does not perceive the transaction as a sporting event, and so does not feel obliged to adhere to the rules, rest every 3 minutes, or even announce their intention to attack. Thus, these arts have their limitations.

7 **Street thug:** At this level, you are playing offensive. You have the skills to look after yourself on the streets. In fact, you love violence, so that becomes the end in itself. Such organisations might attack competitors for the fun of it. They are feared, and generally cause other businesses to simply stay out of their way. This is great for the street thug. However, their lack of focus in respect of their corporate goals, usually means they do not capitalise on the market conditions they have created. Eventually after a brawl too many, they will enter a steep decline.

8 **Mobster:** On the face of it, the mobster is simply a more organised thug. However, they recognise the power of ecosystems/platforms. Taking control of a money supply, be that of a drugs, prostitution or ebooks nature, is the primary objective. It's business, pure and simple. If necessary, alliances will be formed, if they reinforce platform dominance. Violence is considered a waste of resources, but if threatened, full capability will be deployed, and no mercy will be shown.

9 **Ninja:** These sneaky organisations do not advertise. You look down, and your lunch is no longer there. They are pure-play offensive. Skilled assassins. Such organisations target their prey carefully. Unlike a thug, they are not noisy and confrontational. They are already in your camp watching how things work. They are laying contingency traps, should the assassination not go to plan. You will be unaware of the strike when it happens. It could be fatal, or it might just be enough to deliver corporate unconsciousness (think acquisition). Ninjas are skilled healers so they will quickly help the organisation to recover. But that is when the interrogation begins, and they have a variety of questioning techniques, not all of which will be of a civil nature.

Business is moving from the manicured business park to the digital savanna. Like it or not, nature isn't a Walt Disney subsidiary. It is selfish, and often malevolent. Your organisation is either a predator, or prey. Your first job is to assess which one you are, and to then tune your approach accordingly.

** End of post extract **

Enemies old and new

As mentioned, enemies are appearing in new forms. Some organisations are extending up and down their supply chains. Others are moving into adjacent markets to their home territory. There was a time when Silicon Valley entrepreneurs would invite business leaders to lunch with a view to selling their innovative wares. Today the business leaders are the lunch, and the entrepreneurs are less into innovation and more into market domination.

Your august and revered business model might be days away from being in competition with a free app. And at what point does a car embedded with Apple technology have more value being branded an Apple car, rather than retaining its established marque?

Coopetition

Cooperating with competitors is a way to create unique value propositions. Bigger players may find it easier to simply consume smaller competitors. So, best to team up with other players who are not able to dominate the relationship. Though the fintech players have demonstrated that by finding the right niche, you can be small and still call the shots. Extending your tribe by befriending the competition can be a smart move.

Transient monopolies

Monopolies or market leadership in the digital age will be transient at best. Even a radical move, such as leaping from wellington boots maker to becoming the global number one mobile phone player, was not enough to guarantee a sustainable future for one Finnish phone maker. Each day is the start of a new competition. Constant innovation is required. Being ready to abandon your primary business model and hop to one of those you have been nurturing in your polymodal business model portfolio is a requirement. Like the captain of a super luxury cruise liner, you need to ensure that your lifeboats are of a sufficiently high standard, because one of them could become your principle form of transportation.

The new intermediaries

Increasingly value will be unleashed through the incorporation of sensors into traditional offerings. The associated data will form the basis of valuable customer-pleasing insights. I can imagine that this data-driven value will move from the periphery of the offerings to being core for many organisations.

The value of the data will be in proportion to the quality of the associated analytics. The quality of the analytics will be proportional to the data scientists who are set loose on the data.

Unless you are Google or Amazon, or some other data-birthed business, the chances are you might be a little short on data science talent.

Well, Google and Amazon do not have that problem. In fact, they have the capacity to step in as data analysis intermediaries, and thus take a large chunk of what was becoming your primary revenue stream.

I am not suggesting that is what they have in mind regarding your market, or that they might be the only ones. Just be aware that your cool data-driven business model plans might never reach puberty, unless you have factored in this seemingly unfair reality.

Human considerations

- Brace yourself for a talent war. This book is largely about how to put your organisation at an advantage.

- Think carefully about the changing nature of sales, particularly as the focus moves from deal-closing to utilisation. Is there a way that you can make service/sales more social, and thus encourage sharing?

- Plan how you are going to address the data scientist threat I have outlined.

- Brace your people for a rocky ride. Practice 'ship evacuations', so that the business can transform smoothly, should the digital grim reaper turn up at reception.

Capital considerations

- The quality of your engagement with the market (relational capital) will have a positive impact on your human capital. This will have a very direct bearing on your financial capital. Done well, this will create a virtuous circle that will enhance your brand capital, and so lubricate the model further.

- Data capital will facilitate adaptability. Better data leads to a better understanding of the market, and therefore greater visibility of incoming changes ahead.

Take note

- We are back on the savanna. Certainty has given way to volatility, uncertainty, complexity and ambiguity. Our organisation's ability to adapt is critical to survival. There is a reason we no longer see door to door encyclopaedia sellers in the jungle.

- Customers are the prized resource. But unless we are top of the food chain, we are going to have to play very intelligently. And even if we are top of the food chain, that is unlikely to be a permanent arrangement.

- Value creation is increasingly going to be data-originated, which plays into the hands of those organisations that were built with data and the web at their centre. Having a response to this reality will determine your long-term survivability.

10 Added value

Overview

The term 'added value' has several definitions. As a buyer, it can be the difference between what you are willing to pay, and the cost of producing the product yourself/having someone else produce it. Though as a buyer, you would expect the price to be considerably less than the value you are anticipating. It is not unusual for the procurement function of large corporations to tell suppliers that they must demonstrate a ratio of ten to one, or more, in respect of the value their offering will deliver against the price they are proposing.

The added value can also emerge from the brand value of the product or service. Some people will pay a premium to have access to a celebrity lawyer or fitness coach. Their value is not just in their functional capability, but in the social capital that the buyer will enjoy by association. Whether you are a trading tribe or a corporation, your offerings must be clearly value adding.

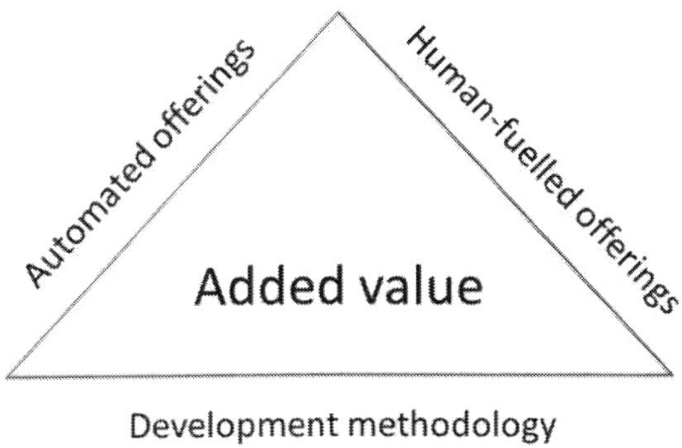

Figure 13 Added value

In this chapter, we are going to explore added value through the lenses of:

- Fully automated offerings.
- Human-fuelled offerings.
- An offerings methodology.

Why is this important…

Our economic relevance hinges on the value of our offerings.

Products v services v utilities

A product can be defined as something that is sold. I might sell you a car, a barrel of cinnamon, or a pint of lager. Once sold, it is yours. Any issues you have, beyond any warranty arrangement, are yours too.

Traditionally a service was intangible. It could be thought of as a product that is created at the point of sale, or more specifically at the point/period of consumption. Your doctor provides a service, as does your security detail. The service might be associated with a given outcome, for example, teach me French, or find me a life partner. Or it may be an ongoing requirement, for example, look after my money, inform me of the weather. The fee model might be:

- Fixed-priced.
  - I pay for the outcome, and have no interest in what costs you incur in the process.
- Time and materials.
  - I pay for your time, however long it takes, and associated expenditure.
- Value-based.
  - I pay you a percentage of the value that your service creates for my organization.
- Utility
  - I pay for what I use.

Fixed-priced works well when you want to limit your financial risk. Value-based works well when you want to incentivise your supplier to become more of a partner. Time and materials generally doesn't work, and is only used when the buyer has vague requirements, for example, we need a software developer, but not sure for how long. Traditionally some unscrupulous service companies pushed for T&M contracts because they essentially turned their worst performing people into their most profitable. Their people typically moved with sloth-like dynamism. Utility works well for commodity services, where the requirement may vary based on, for example, weather or customer demand.

It is also worth noting that products are increasingly morphing into services. Rather than buy the car, and thus also acquire the servicing responsibility, we buy a car service. Whether we need a car for an hour, a day or three years, we know that the amount we pay factors in the service costs. This is attractive from a cash flow perspective as product purchases can cause cashflow perturbations. Also, products tend to be depreciating assets. When I buy a computer server, I am likely paying the peak price, given the tendency for computer hardware to drop in price over time. And given the likelihood that I will not be using it to its full capacity on day one, I will be paying this premium, but only enjoying a fraction of its value.

As mentioned, there is a trend towards everything as a service. Water, gas and electricity are traditional utility services. Increasingly, this model is being embraced by the tech sector, thanks to the cloud (aka the web), where we can now rent infrastructure and access to applications.

Whilst some of us might enjoy the self-expression that comes with acquiring a bespoke solution, the market is pushing us towards a utility model. As a digital leader in say a professional services firm, you need to think about how you turn your high value strategic consultancy, audit or tax offering into a mobile app. Or at least, make it accessible in a low fuss, low cost, quick response manner. I am, in fact, suggesting that you cannibalise your business model. You can wait to see what your competitors intend, or you can be first to market. You will be trading margin for volume, but that is also a trend in the digital age.

Whilst you might not use the tagline, 'high value services, at grubby prices', that's the business many of us will be in.

Value creation

Value is not a universally understood concept. Much of my work over the years has been in helping IT leaders increase their strategic relevance. Part of that exercise was in moving their boardroom conversations from a focus on costs to a focus on value. When CIOs struggle to articulate their initiatives and budget requests in respect of business value, the conversation quickly reverts to cost.

The CFO needs to put a number in a spreadsheet in order to add that number to other numbers, and to compare that number to other numbers. As an aside, please note, for those of you considering a career as a CFO, this is not an exhaustive list of the associated responsibilities. CFOs like cost, because it is unambiguous and easy to manage.

In some cases, the conversation evolves, and terms such as return on investment are used, and cost of opportunity. These of course are still cost and not value measures.

The real issue is who is responsible for value creation. In my view, the IT function cannot take responsibility for the business value of the systems and services they provide, any more than they can make a commitment to ensure the company's stock will hit a certain price. Often the value in IT services comes about through the way those services are exploited by the users. At best, value creation is a shared responsibility across the business as a whole.

For the purposes of defining value within the organisation, I would suggest that anything that supports the achievement of the organisation's strategic imperatives is value creating. In my view, the strategic imperatives are to increase the value of the five capital pots that form part of the Biz 4.0 model. This value definition also applies to the value organisations might supply to other organisations.

For the purposes of defining value for consumers, I would suggest that any product or service that enables the consumer to be more human is value creating. Think back to our nine anthropological drivers. How can our offerings support the natural desire to be mobile, social, creative, and so on. And of course, how can these be supported to also contribute to the human capital goals of enterprise buyers. Productivity offerings that 'give us back time' are increasingly valuable, as people wake up to the preciousness of life. Services that do not drain our cognitive capacity will also be attractive. The less clicks the better.

Life's fundamentals, food, shelter and clothing will always be in demand. We also need to consider the emotional needs that drive our perception of value. Six areas that have been identified by famed motivational author and speaker Anthony Robbins, as being the most important. These include, our desire:

- To contribute, and be seen to be contributing.
- For certainty and comfort.
- For uncertainty and variety.
- For significance.
- For love and connection.
- For personal growth.

Providing services that can clearly cause an uptick on any of the personal or enterprise metrics mentioned can be considered as value-adding.

Digital age value

Data

We have already identified how data can be used to boost the value our buyers receive from our offerings. Health trackers are really wristwatches that with a few embedded sensors can provide the user with valuable personal information.

IoT has the potential to boost the value proposition of everything from cutlery to clothing.

Data-driven value can deepen customer relationships.

Imagine a car breakdown provider whose services requires the insertion of sensors in the customer's car. This sensor can provide real-time car health analytics. It can also provide driver quality data, which in itself might be indicative of wider health issues. But the sensors, working in conjunction with other car sensors, could develop maps depicting road quality that could be used as part of the satellite navigation functionality to present the smoothest routes, ie. those that will take the least toll on the car. So, there is value in both personalised and collated data.

Social

The idea of sharing how slowly I ran a few miles last night seems an unlikely functional 'must have'. But I must admit that the online element of my running activities really has added to the quality of my running, primarily through making it a more social activity. So, building online sociality into products and services appears to be a real value add. Being able to engage with other fellow tractor purchasers, in essence, turns your customer base into your service desk.

What about Tinder for airplanes? I am not referring to an optimised process for joining the 'mile high club', but a mechanism to enable people to get together for social/professional purposes. Passengers have the option to make their presence known to other passengers on the flight. They would identify their professional and personal interests, and whether they would like to meet likeminded people before, during, or after the flight.

For shy users, they could anonymise their profile, and just communicate using the app. Or they could arrange for a physical meeting. Perhaps a perk might be that the airline arranges the seating such that likeminded people sit together. Possibly my proposed name for this social travel offering might need revisiting?

Collaborative consumption

Providing a framework that enables, for example, purchasers of your power tools to share the tool with occasional users would be very valuable. Possibly the owner might make some money by hiring it out. Your company gains brand exposure through this reduced risk 'trial access' to your products. Perhaps in the past, only the wealthy could afford your product. What if you provided a framework that enabled less wealthy people to make a group purchase, along with the ability to share usage on a basis that reflects the percentage contribution? Cars come to mind.

Access

Luxury goods are exclusive by design. So why not create a private online club where admittance is limited to your best clients? Luxury product consultants can provide content by way of articles and live clinics. Forums will enable the well-heeled to swap notes on what is important to them. By combining online scheduling with the traditional Tupperware party model, the vendor could encourage its community to gather together in the physical world. Perhaps in an upmarket restaurant that would see value in being a proposed venue. Data and collaborative technologies have the potential to unleash dormant vaults of value for your customers.

Fully automated offerings

Attractiveness

Fully automated offerings have a lot going for them. Some people would rather not engage with a commission-seeking assistant, preferring to peruse the 'store' at their leisure. Plus, there is a lot to be said for being able to make purchases with just a few clicks. Cloud-based services also enable the customer to buy or consume when and where it suits them.

As drones become more integrated into the supply chain, everything from milk to coal will be purchased and delivered without any human intervention. People are offering their spare rooms at home to suppliers for use as part of a distributed distribution centre. The book you have in mind to buy might be sitting next door (next store?). The pressure is on to move from next day delivery to immediate gratification.

Virtual assistants will increasingly harness the power of AI to handle purchases that have a degree of fuzziness. This might include:

- Booking taxis, trains and planes in respect to getting to a destination by a set time, factoring in the personal preferences of the traveller.
- Creating a shortlist of candidate CFOs based on the financial history of the organisation, and the composition of the leadership team.
- Manage either a corporate or personal wealth portfolio, based on pre-stated goals.

Not everyone today would be comfortable with trusting technology with tasks that have so much potential to go wrong. But given the time-pressure buyers are facing, this sort of sophisticated delegation will prove very attractive. Over time, it is likely that we will wonder how we ever trusted humans to carry out such delicate tasks.

Evolving models

The likes of Netflix and Amazon have started to offer 'all you can eat' service buffets. You pay a flat fee, which is typically so low that it wouldn't be the first thing you would drop if you had to recalibrate your spending. And for that low flat fee, you can gorge yourself senseless. Most people are familiar with the Netflix model. Amazon has a service called Kindle Unlimited, which provides unlimited access to a select set (well over a million) of e-books. Some authors would regard Kindle Unlimited as a mechanism for transferring value from the author to the reader, which for many authors is painful.

The beauty of a fully automated online service is that it is possible to have an infinitely large store. With such a store, there is money to be made in the 'long tail', ie. those books that only sell very occasionally. Physical bookstores optimise their limited space by stocking only those books that sold well. Online stores, unburdened by retail space limitations, can exploit the opportunity that comes with offering an infinite catalogue comprising books with low associated sales volumes. A few sales per book times many books adds up to a lot of sales. The concept was documented by former Wired editor, Chris Anderson, in his book of the same name. The tagline, 'why the future of business is selling less of more' captures the essence of the model.

As some young consumers enter the corporate world, they have certain expectations in respect of how they acquire and consume services. This will push enterprises towards iconised/store-like interfaces, where the users access corporate services as if they were consumer services. A typical characteristic of a consumerised service is the way it is simplified/dumbed down. Functionality is sometimes traded for ease of use. Compare an iPad keyboard to that of a corporate laptop to see this from a hardware perspective.

Humans as exception handlers

As a generally happy Amazon user, I have no real idea as to whether there are any humans involved in customer-services. If there are, I have no idea as to how to contact them when my orders do not on occasion arrive on time. As we transition to full automation, it is likely that humans may hang in there in the capacity of 'exception handlers'. Transactions that befuddle the technology will be routed through to a human. But each exception will become a 'case' that the intelligent software will eventually recognise, and so over time will not need to involve a human.

We have come a long way in this respect. Who would have thought at the inception of restaurants that one day there would be a need to self-serve, or even take the food away to consume elsewhere? Having your meal produced by a robot and delivered by a drone isn't far off.

But possibly 3D printing/cooking appliances will be a more energy efficient approach. So, the world's top/most popular chefs can move out of the food construction business and into the software business.

Every time you opt for a signature dish, you will find yourself paying for the materials, but also paying for the 'one off' use of the chef's meal algorithm. This is human capital repurposed for the digital age.

Human-fuelled offerings

Humans have justified a role in the workplace by being able to do things that technology was unable to do. The options in this respect are narrowing by the hour.

So, let's look at the role humans will continue to play, for the foreseeable at least, in the digital age.

Three levels of human involvement

Person-centric: In this case, the client is buying the capabilities of an individual. We must have Usain Bolt, Frank Sinatra or Picasso. There are no substitutes. Somebody who looks like Usain Bolt, and is pretty fast, will not draw the crowds to your 'night of the stars' track meet. Increasingly your top talent will fall into this category. Having them in your camp will be part of the value proposition of your offerings.

Professional-centric: Here the market wants someone who is professionally competent, whether that be a doctor, lawyer or technology consultant. They need to be able to apply initiative to the task, and this is what makes them a preferable option to a technology solution. However, we don't need a specific individual. If I am having my appendix removed, I don't need the best surgeon in the world to handle this. A competent and qualified surgeon will suffice.

Cog-centric: A human is required, but the role doesn't really require the person to unleash their full cerebral capacity. This might involve the delivery of post, manning a call centre or washing hair.

The cogs are clearly at more risk of automation than those who are uniquely talented. You are encouraged to look at your talent pool in the light of this classification, and using new technology reshape your talent profile to reflect a focus on uniquely skilled people. This might seem cruel. But it is necessary. Organisations with a social conscience will help the cog workers upskill to professional class. Such a policy will likely prove attractive to many top-end artists looking to work at organisations with a heart.

The rise of product geniuses

Again, when it comes to the retail experience, many of us would rather avoid the clutches of a weaponised sales professional. How pleasant it is to enter an Apple store and peruse at your leisure. Should you have a question, one of the store's 'geniuses' will happily answer your questions with the carefree indifference of someone who is not commission-based. And they will do so purely for the thrill of articulating their genius.

What we are likely to see is the evolution of the retail store from being a place where goods are sold to being a centre of product experience, expertise and evangelism. So, if we consider the car sales process. In the past, with great reluctance, the potential buyer would have to visit the showroom multiple times. Some visits might involve a test drive, discussion of the commercials, queries about functionality and so on. Today much of this can be done online, including car personalisation. So, the reason for visiting the showroom is to experience the car. Cars are pretty much guaranteed to perform as advertised, consequently, even the need to take a test drive is not strictly necessary. Unless of course, you are likely to be using it in an unconventional manner, for example, competitive point to point cross country caravanning,

That sinking feeling you experience as you sense a rapidly approaching 'retail shark' will be no more, given that the commercial aspects will be handled online. The only people at the showroom will be the product geniuses.

In fact, these product geniuses might well be former mechanics who have acquired deep knowledge by getting their hands dirty. The less sharp-suited they look the better. I am nervous of people who specialise in human manipulation, particularly those who wear the spoils of their commissions as a badge of honour. To me, the more hands-on and oily the expert looks, the better. This genius phenomenon, again points to service being the new sales.

In any case, the role of product/service expert is likely to grow, as the role of sales professional declines.

The race to the bottom

I have already mentioned how the banks are in a 'race to the bottom' in respect of automation. Once they hit 'commodity rock bottom', they will likely start to reemploy humans. These humans will need to be highly creative artists. They will also be geniuses, though not necessarily of the Apple customer-facing kind. For the foreseeable future, humans will provide the cognitive power that will fuel forthcoming innovations.

Again, we will see a surge in human-powered offerings. The offerings themselves may well be fully automated, but their conception took place in someone's head, or through the collaboration of multiple heads. AI-based technologies will no doubt play a part in boosting the cognitive capabilities of the humans. Offerings created by 'augmented humans' will grow in the next few years. It is only when the technology can do what humans do will we see the withdrawal of people from the workplace. It is a little early to mention this, but it is inevitable.

The good news is that humans will continue to have a role to play in respect of product/service creation, and delivery. But our role will require that we use our brains in a manner that many of us will find taxing. Most of us arrive home mentally exhausted not because we have spent eight plus hours in a hyper-focused creative trance, but because we have spent the day wading through red tape, mopping up the messes of careless colleagues, or sitting in pointless power play meetings.

Humans are most welcome to the digital age party. All guests must arrive with a fully-serviced brain, and the expectation that they will be expected to use it.

Offerings methodology

Adding value can happen by chance. Perhaps, you have observed trends in Internet-streamed music. You have also noticed that even the most rural of areas in your country have wireless broadband. Equipped with these insights, you set up a musical tractor factory. Months before the first products roll off the conveyor belt, you commission some big budget TV and printed media ads.

And as luck would have it, your hunch pays off. And now Apple wants a piece of this, and is offering to provide discounted country music to your growing tribe of sonic agriculturalists. This is of course quite unlikely. Two or more plausible observations are not necessarily indicative of a market opportunity. Sometimes people will start a business based on a personal interest, or based on something that is in keeping with the needs of their ego. This is why most businesses fail.

Capital-intensive businesses, such as musical tractors, will fail at scale. Most start-up businesses, or even established businesses, do not have the budget to convince the market that there is a need for this new offering. Typically, the market wants something that it can easily conceptualise, "so, it's a car, but can drive itself", "it's like a book, but is accessible via a reading device", "it's like an iPod, but with massive wheels and power steering". Only the likes of Apple can take a concept such as a tablet, "It's like a laptop, but with most of the functionality stripped out", and make it a market success.

Most us needs to be a little more circumspect before investing capital, including our life force, in new ventures. This requires more than simply polling those you know. Even if they are representative of your target market, they may not have the heart to tell you that your idea is just another vanity project, whose only redeeming feature is its likely short lifespan.

You might even commission some market research involving focus groups to study the attitudes and behaviours of your target market in respect of your prospective product. But we live in a world where what people say in the comfort of a focus group is not necessarily reflective of whether they would part with money back out in the digital savanna. The only true test of a product's market viability is to put it into the market and see what happens.

Entrepreneur, Eric Ries, recognised this issue, and through his understanding of the Japanese concept of lean manufacturing developed a methodology that could be applied to start-up businesses. His book, entitled, 'The Lean Startup', nails the most efficient and risk-free approach to growing a new business. So, I won't repeat his approach. But the key messages are that you should:

- Get something into the market at your first opportunity. It may be a shadow of what you have in mind, but it will give the market something to sniff and possibly chew on. Ries talks of the minimum viable product (MVP).
- Study how the market responds with rapt attention. Is there a steady growth in website visits? What does the qualitative feedback suggest? Has the press picked up on this? Has anyone actually bought one?
- Based on this data, you either add more functionality, change the existing functionality, or abandon the project.

For me, the beauty of this approach is that it removes the luck aspect of product development, and turns this exercise into a simple set of procedures to be managed. No gut feelings, purely data-driven.

The Lean Startup was written with growing a business in mind. But it is equally valid to evolving new products and services. It doesn't obviate the need for investment, and doesn't protect against financial loss, but it does manage the associated risks in an effective manner; assuming your decision making is based on a suitable data sample size.

The Attention success factor we have explored is key to this process.

In the Ambition success factor chapter, I mentioned the need to run your business like a portfolio of experiments. More specifically, this is a portfolio of added-value experiments. Your organisation will increasingly resemble a laboratory with different embryonic products and services gestating (in the market). Their vital signs being the market data you capture. Some experiments might be functional variants of an established value-added offering. Some experiments will explore business model variants. Once you have established that the market likes what you have in mind, the question now is whether:

- The market gets it for free. You make money on the advertising opportunities.
- You charge a on-off premium price to differentiate it from similar offerings.
- You charge many of your customers at below cost, but compensate for this by charging a small price-insensitive group a premium price. For example, the people who need to get to their destination at the first opportunity, so they are willing to pay a premium price, even on a budget airline flight.
- You incentivise the influencers to use your offering, and in turn become brand ambassadors.
- You encourage illegal usage of your service, so that it gains viral-like market momentum. Once critical mass is reached, you can patch the 'fault'/get legal.

And the way to decide which of these is the best way forward is to try them all. It may turn out that you use them all, but their usage may be seasonally, geographically or demographically driven.

Human considerations

- Humans are going to continue to be an important part of creating and delivering value adding services and products. But, in most cases, we are going to have to raise our game significantly.

- Products and services that support our anthropological drivers will have natural appeal. In the enterprise, personal productivity and collaboration technologies reflect this.
- Given how formulaic creating new services is becoming, thanks to the Lean Startup approach, I would expect to see an explosion in entrepreneurial activity in the coming years. Much of this will emerge from garages and bedrooms of unfunded experimenters. Smart organisations will develop a means to identify such innovation and nurture it with a view to helping all parties win.
- It is likely your future products and services will increasingly emerge from the informal experimentation of your people, rather than through some industrialised R&D function. Companies such as Google recognise the value in letting their people follow their curiosity.

Capital considerations

- One would expect that the act of providing added value to customers would have a positive impact on financial capital, presuming the capital inflows were in excess to the cost of running the business.

- An in-demand array of products and services will have a positive impact on brand capital. Overall brand equity being the sum of the equity associated with each offering.

- Intellectual property will be boosted by the creation of value adding services, particularly where the services are not dependent on the need for specific individuals in the delivery process. But as we move to a world where it is the very involvement of a specific high profile, talented individual that has given rise to the offerings attractiveness, it is likely that some of the associated intellectual capital generated will have to be shared with that talented individual.

Take note

- Businesses exist to create value for their markets. Talented people similarly want to create value for the market. The organisations that are the most obsessed with creating value will likely attract the most value-obsessed talent. Conversely, indifferent organisations will attract indifferent people. Together they will spiral into the commercial abyss.

- Humans are key to value creation in the digital age, but only if their brains are engaged. Process work will be largely done by technology. Talented people in the digital age will develop the skills to harness new technologies. This includes using AI-fueled analytics tools, and co-working harmoniously with robots.

- Understanding what value creation means to your market is very important. Consumers value offerings that:

  - Save them time.
  - Do not consume their cognitive capacity unnecessarily.
  - Make them more productive/successful/healthy/attractive.
  - Make the world a better place.
    - Or at least minimise making it worse.

11 Next steps

Overview

You are now familiar with the elements of the Biz 4.0 blueprint (think 5-9-5). Next, we will look at how you can approach transforming your business with that in mind.

We will also look at some of the important business issues that we have not explicitly addressed in the blueprint.

This is important because...

Industrial era organisations cannot afford to operate in a 'business as usual' manner, and so taking steps towards transformation is critical to staying economically relevant in the digital age.

Next steps - start-up

The following steps are suggested for start-up organisations. The presumption being that the start-up is either just a conceptual idea at this stage, or is operational, but has yet to establish a profitable set of offerings.

Start-ups are encouraged to approach the implementation of the success factors in the following order:

1. Attention.
2. Ambition.
3. Added value.
4. Artistry.
5. Adaptability.

Let's explore these in more detail:

Attention

It is important to have a clear understanding of the market, particularly in respect of how it is responding to your product/service prototypes (MVPs). The insights that you will learn from paying attention are fundamental to each step you take. So, getting the sensor and decision making machinery in place is the top priority.

Ambition

Developing a sense of purpose in respect of why the business exists needs to be established very early on to ensure the founders are in alignment, so to speak. Any disagreements can be resolved quickly, rather than being left to fester only to surface later when they could materially disrupt the organisation's growth. Now is a good time to think about weaving in cultural norms and innovation into the organisational fabric, before you start to recruit. This will be difficult/impossible to do once the head count starts to mount.

Added value

This is a critical element of the start up process. The associated processes need to commence as soon as possible. The venture begins in earnest once the market gains exposure to your embryonic offerings. The sooner you discover you are on the right track, the sooner you can ramp up the business. The sooner you discover it is not quite what the market wants, the sooner you can try a modified approach, or, if appropriate, shut down the experiment without further incursion of cost.

Artistry

Whilst, I have laboured the importance of talent, and its importance to business success in the digital age, it is likely that the early product development will be carried out by the founders, and so the business of talent attraction and retention will not be the top priority.

Nonetheless, it would be wise to put the 'machinery' in place prior to the talent influx.

Adaptability

Adaptability is key to survival. One could argue that this is the first job of any start-up. Surely, only after looking at the macroeconomic indicators, market potential and competitors should one even consider embarking on a start-up venture?

My concern with this is that it presumes that you know with some precision that there is a market for your offering. But you are unlikely to know this if you have yet to test it in the market. In depth market analysis prior to introducing a new offering is a very 'industrial era' approach. Of course, you have a sense of what you will offer the market, but you might discover quite early on that the market likes where you are going, but has a very different view as to how your offering will be used. For example:

- Your non-cellular emergency service communication offering might be rejected by the emergency services, but embraced by theme parks and universities.
- Your specialist online dating app is gaining great traction in the health industry, where the growing army of freelance health therapists need a platform to share best practice and source people in need of their services.
- Your quantified-self smart body stocking, designed for elite athletes, has become a de rigor fashion accessory amongst fans of electronic dance music.

I am not suggesting that you do not do any initial research. Just be aware of its limited value. Nothing is more accurate than the market's economic response to your offerings. Once you have established that you have something attractive to sell, then you can ramp up customer and competitor activity, and plot your journey in the context of macroeconomic trends.

This ordering is just a recommendation. Your circumstances may necessitate a reordering. A suboptimal success factors implementation plan will not be catastrophic, but it could make your venture unnecessarily risky and bumpy.

There will always be some degree of reverse engineering, as this is a natural part of running your business in 'permanently in beta' mode. But there is no point setting yourself up for unnecessary reengineering, if you can avoid it. Thus, it would be wise to give consideration as to what the optimal implementation order would be for your unique set of circumstances.

Next steps – established organisation

The following steps are recommended for established organisations, ie. those that have an established cash flow:

1. Attention.
2. Adaptability.
3. Ambition.
4. Artistry.
5. Added value.

Attention

If you do not have great sensitivity in respect of what is happening in the market, then this needs to be a priority. Otherwise you are just flying blind, with no sense as to whether changes in direction are for the better.

It is likely that you have an established workforce, but possibly they are more cog workers than artists. In any case, ensuring that your people are not being drained of their cognitive capacity by virtue of poor organisational design must be a priority. Even if your people are focused on process work, you do not want to lose them because of poor management, unnecessary red tape and so on.

Adaptability

If you haven't been paying attention to your clients, competitors and the macroeconomic trends, then you are again flying blind. The sooner you can assess your situation, and continue to assess your situation, the better. Are you haemorrhaging clients? Are you conscious of the growing scarcity of raw materials critical to your offerings? Unlike a start-up, you are presiding over a tribe that has something to lose. Thus, you must be very aware of the terrain in which you are operating.

Ambition

Now that the organisation has a better understanding of its current predicament, it can think about how it might move forward. Some established organisations have a culture by default, rather than by design. Some organisations see innovation as something that is confined to an R&D function.

It is not simply a case of reengineering the culture to that of an innovation dream team. That's unlikely to happen with somnambulant process workers. My recommendation is not to tinker with the existing operational model, because it represents your primary cash flow. Any such reengineering does not come with a cast iron guarantee of organisational success. Though it does come with a high likelihood of operational disruption, and probably failure.

So, I suggest that all your cultural/innovation energies are directed towards your plan b, c, d etc. models. Remember polymodal business? You need to think about how you evolve into a risk-apportioned portfolio of experiments. Will you buy a few start-ups? Or bring in some high-quality talent and offer them a blank canvas?

Artistry

Once the new portfolio businesses start to gain some traction, you will need to populate them with talented people. This requires a whole new level of talent management, and so you need to be sure that your current HR function is capable of this leap.

It might well be that you leave the current HR function as it is, on the basis that plan A, your (current) primary business model, needs cog worker management capability.

For your growth businesses, I would suggest outsourcing all the administrative aspects of HR, and to hold the plan b, c, d etc. leaders responsible for artistry acquisition matters. Over time, you might extend your procurement department to have a section dedicated to the commodity aspects of talent management. This will not include engagement with talent agencies, as that will be a leadership responsibility.

One should always be on the look out for 'plan a' cog workers who feel they would thrive in one of the new business experiments. Just to clarify, I am not intending to deride industrial era workers by using the term cog workers. My point is that through industrial era schooling and employment expectations, many workers have had their creative 'gene' turned off. But as the new world of work becomes more visible, some cog workers might well feel an emotional attraction to this new way of working that requires full brain engagement. We should welcome these people because if they are motivated to make the transition, there is a good chance it will be successful.

Added value

Your organisation is already adding value. The concern is for how long will the current offerings be in demand. Each of the emerging business models associated with your polymodal business approach will be underpinned by one or more new offerings. Ensuring that these are evolving using a data-driven lean start-up approach will be important.

Your offerings will constitute a blend of human and technology capability. Maximising the potential of both 'ingredients' will be key to your success.

Again, your circumstances may necessitate a reordering of the implementation of these success factors. Though, as an established organisation with greater resources than a start-up, you may be able to parallel process their implementation.

It may be that for one reason or another you have already tackled/started the transition in respect to one or more of these success factors. Build on what you have built.

An important consideration is that you must not press ahead with the transition until you have alerted your people as to what your intentions are. In the main, your current people will not be affected, as the aim is to minimise disruption of existing cash flows.

You don't need their agreement or blessing, but it would do no harm to ensure that everybody understands why this is happening. Some people are so bogged down in work and life that they do not see the digital tsunami approaching.

Smart organisations will not protect the workers from this reality, but will proactively develop resources and tools to help their people make their personal transition to a digital future. Of course, they will need to be amenable to making the leap.

Wider considerations

The Biz 4.0 blueprint addresses the key elements of a digital age business. But there are some areas that require special attention. We will look at these now:

Governance

Corporate governance, including risk management and regulatory compliance are a reality. The Biz 4.0 blueprint might seem a little too reckless in the context of large fines and suspension from trading. The reality is that failure (aka active learning) is an important aspect of digital age business. Regulators, investors and analysts need to wake up to this. I would hope that as organisations become more data-driven, their ability to manage the downside will improve. Avoiding the sunk costs fallacy by looking at the numbers will hopefully lead to improved financial governance.

In my work with regulators, I am seeing them start to take a lean start-up approach in respect of developing new rules. Smart organisations will look to work with the regulators, rather than work out how to how to avoid detection/fulfil the minimum technical requirements. You are both in the business of serving the market. I suggest you approach this as a team.

Security

Information security is a well-established, and growing concern. The use of intelligent embedded devices will ramp up the entry points for hackers. But even the most secure 'edge' technology will do little to protect the organisation if people are part of your business model.

How many of your people have a password such as 'password' or 12345678? Perhaps some use 'incorrect', so that if they forget, the device will remind them what it is. It's not just an issue of password management, but of having a security-oriented mindset.

A security policy induction programme for new entrants makes sense. But increasingly your workforce will largely comprise transient project-based talent, who perhaps might be with you for only a month, or perhaps the first Wednesday of each month.

I am not suggesting that freelancers are a risk and your established permanent workers are not. Perhaps the former see security mindfulness as an important part of their brand, and so are very aware of their responsibilities in this respect. Whether permanent or not, highly distracted people can fall prey to, for example, spear phishing attacks.

Improving the overall attention capabilities of your organisation including, for example, threat detection, will help. As will the cognitive reclamation work you do to stop people feeling overwhelmed and distracted. This does not constitute a security policy, but it does lay the foundations for ensuring that your security policy will be internalised.

Mergers and acquisitions

M&A is a reality, particularly in markets that are hosting ecosystem endgame competitions, and is a natural part of the polymodal business approach. Acquiring other organisations will potentially act as an insurance policy against the failure of your primary business. In my experience, there are rarely mergers of equals. There is typically the Pacman and the pac-dots. If you are the acquirer, then be clear as to whether you are asset stripping, for example, the intellectual property or the client list. Or if you intend to nurture the acquired business, you are encouraged to not tinker with the culture, unless you want to create a stampede amongst the acquired staff.

Whilst it is tempting to splat your branding over the acquired business, and tame the founder, try to avoid it. The point of the acquisition is to introduce new business genes to the business, rather than embalm the acquisition for the journey across the 'River Styx' with your primary business when the digital Grim Reaper signs in at reception.

Supply chain management

Supply chain management (SCM) might be considered an unglamorous part of business. 'Front of house' is where the action takes place, and the experience is created. I hear very little of the 'supplier journey'. We should be aware that in many respects, SCM is where we will see the most radical aspects of digital disruption, for example:

- The shift from manufacturing in the factory to in the home via 3D printers.
- The use of IoT in changing the relationship between the factory machinery and the materials being processed.
- The increasing connectivity between the consumer and the manufacturer in respect of personalisation.
- The use of driverless vehicles and drones in respect of logistics.
- The use of social media to drive production targets.

Market volatility coupled with customer fickleness will make it tough for all but the most digitally-smart suppliers.

Smart organisations will evolve their procurement functions such that price is not the only metric. So hopefully, it will be goodbye to those procurement staff who behave more like professional sadists who enjoy beating suppliers to within 'an inch of their lives'. As the race for ecosystem dominance accelerates, it is likely that suppliers and their buyers will move to a more entwined partnership model where risk is more evenly shared, as is reward.

Suppliers impact all five of the success factors. As such, they require an appropriate level of leadership attention, and respect.

Legal

Your legal team, particularly if you preside over an industrial era model, will squirm at the changes I am proposing. But like the rest of us, they need to speed up, reassess their value proposition, and become more comfortable with risk. Much of law lends itself to AI. We will still require humans for legal engineering, but that will be for exceptional circumstances only. Young lawyers will be relieved at this shift. No more donkeywork. But the likelihood is that we will need fewer lawyers.

Unless you are breaking new ground legally on a regular basis, you might be better served by a third-party law firm. Ideally one with a utility service model.

PR

Public relations specialists are going to be hit hard by the digital age. Talented people are not going to have their tweets and other social outbursts mediated by the 'messaging police'. It is painful to witness the tweets of very bright people who are clearly being very careful to stay within some predefined corporate code of communication. Increasingly, your corporate message is no longer under your control. This is the problem when you allow real humans into your organisation. And that is another reason why the industrial era was not so keen on human nature.

Talented individuals in the digital age arrive with their own following. Thus, there is no need for PR specialists to ensure that market opinion leaders are kept up to speed with your organisation's developments. This is because your talent will be the opinion leaders. PR professionals need to reassess their value proposition.

CSR

An organisation's corporate social responsibility policies reflect its values and standards in respect of all stakeholders, not just shareholders. Smart organisations recognise that this is much more than a tick box exercise. Digital age talent, by choosing to work with your organisation, is exposing itself to your brand. Your brand, which in part is coloured by your CSR approach, needs to offer the talent a brand uplift by association, and not the other way around. Your CSR approach is going to be a key element of your talent acquisition and retention strategy. Be aware that some critics regard CSR as a distraction from the business of doing business, and is simply window dressing that has no economic value. This is very industrial age thinking.

Post-worker society

Many industries have already felt the cold winds of automation. Many more will. There will come a point where there is very little need for humans to be involved in work, because the robots will be able to do everything we can do, only better, with less fuss, and cheaper.

It may be that governments introduce the concept of 'busywork' to give people a sense that they are useful, even though their activity is yielding little by way of economic value. Perhaps organisations will be obliged to involve humans in a certain percentage of their revenue generating activities. This wrinkle in their automated business model might be ameliorated with attractive corporate tax allowances.

The Biz 4.0 blueprint does not guarantee a future for humans in the workplace, but it does lay out an approach to keeping humans in play by maximising their own capability using new technologies.

Take note

- The manner in which you embrace the Biz 4.0 blueprint will likely be determined by both your organisation's chronological and anthropological maturity. If your organisation has treated its people as task-driven worker cogs, then it would be better to start a parallel business (or three – remember the polymodal approach), than trying to repair your culture, and empower your people.

- In my experience, once distrust is built into the employer-employee relationship, any attempt by the employer to become more people-friendly will just be perceived as management weakness, and something to be exploited by the employees. Similarly empowering them with autonomy and the option to be creative will unsettle them, as they will have become institutionally helpless, reliant on their boss to make the decisions.

- Whether you embrace the Biz 4.0 blueprint in full, or in part, you need to ensure that all important aspects of your business are retained. Whilst the game is becoming faster and riskier, we cannot simply sacrifice, for example, governance. But we do need to redefine every aspect of our business to reflect the realities of the post-industrial world.

Afterword

The Biz 4.0 blueprint is not just another attempt to shoehorn management theory onto reality. It seeks to capitalise on our true nature, so that people feel more fulfilled, and businesses, and societies, thrive.

The application of the Biz 4.0 blueprint to your organisation is very much dependent on your organisation's maturity, and the extent to which you buy into its underlying premises:

1. Businesses exist to create value for their stakeholders, of which shareholders are a subset.
2. If we consider the business as a tribe, and develop a tribal mindset, we will be in a better position to thrive in the digital age.
3. Humans have certain anthropological drivers that, if met, will increase their engagement with the business.

I would not expect to receive much pushback in respect of my perspectives on value, nor on the anthropological drivers I have flagged. But I appreciate that the success factors might well be up for discussion. Though even these are based on tribal behavior that has been extremely stress tested over a substantial period.

If you are considering how you might take this forward and do not like my success factors, then, at the very least, I would strongly encourage you to put your people at the centre of your business, be very sensitive to what is happening both inside and outside your organisation, and be highly adaptable to the vagaries of the market.

Most people are unaware of what is happening, and how the world will change, as we transition into the digital age. I hope you will have developed a sense of what lies ahead from reading this book. Most of us will feel some sense of discomfort. Like the sound of a breaking twig at night, that feeling might save your skin.

I am on a mission to alert people as to what lies ahead. Many are behaving as if tomorrow will be the same as yesterday, 'business as usual'. It will be too late when the tsunami is upon them; perhaps boiled frog would be a better metaphor. In any case, the sooner people are warned, the sooner they can take ownership of their future. As a business leader, you are in a strong position to raise the alarm, and lead your people to the digital high ground.

In reading this book, you are likely ahead of the game, at least in awareness of what lies ahead, what is driving the future, and the actions you need to take. In the spirit of the Biz 4.0 blueprint, I encourage you to make nature your business partner.

Thank you for your attention.

Ade McCormack

Appendix A: References

Overview

Here is a list of sources, comprising books and online articles, I have used directly and indirectly in this book.

You can access the online references below, including the Amazon links to the books, by visiting:

www.ademccormack.com/digitalstrategy/biz-4/resources/

The List

McCormack, A. 2017. **Attention Dynamics: High personal performance in the digital age.** Auridian Press.

McCormack, A. 2015. **Beyond Nine to Five: Your career guide for the digital age.** Auridian Press.

Csikszentmihalyi, M. 2013. **Flow: The psychology of happiness.** Ebury Digital.

Levitt, S. 2007. **Freakonomics: A rogue economist explores the hidden side of everything.** Penguin.

Ries, E. 2011. **The Lean Startup: How constant innovation creates radically successful businesses.** Portfolio Penguin.

Blawatt, K. 2016. **Narconomics: How to run a drug cartel.** Ebury Press.

Ericsson, A. and Pool, R. 2016. **Peak: How all of us can achieve extraordinary things.** Vintage Digital.

Tzu, S. 2010. **The Art of War.** Capstone.

Gratton, L. and Scott, A. 2016. **The Hundred Year Life: Living and working in an age of longevity.** Bloomsbury Business.

Peppers, D. 1998. **The One to One Future: Building relationships one customer at a time.** Bantam Doubleday Dell Publishing Group.

Maister, D. et al. 2002. **The Trusted Advisor.** Simon and Schuster.

Junger, S. 2016. **Tribe: On homecoming and belonging.** Fourth Estate.

Thiel, P. and Masters, B. 2014. **Zero to One: Notes on Start Ups, or how to build the future.** Virgin Digital.

Online

10 innovative organisations:
http://www.industryweek.com/innovation/10-most-innovative-companies-world most

Adaptability:
http://anthro.palomar.edu/adapt/adapt_2.htm

Adaptability: The new competitive advantage:
http://www.themanager.org/2015/01/adaptability-new-competitive-advantage/

Artistry and skills:
http://www.survivalinternational.org/galleries/ingenious

Analytics 3.0:
https://hbr.org/2013/12/analytics-30

Apple – A simple product line:
http://www.edibleapple.com/2009/02/03/why-a-simple-product-line-is-integral-to-apples-success/

Augmented humanity:
http://www.forbes.com/sites/sap/2016/12/01/idc-2017-predictions-birth-of-augmented-humanity/

Automation and the future of work:
http://www.mckinsey.com/global-themes/employment-and-growth/automation-jobs-and-the-future-of-work

Automation of knowledge jobs:
https://hbr.org/2016/06/the-knowledge-jobs-most-likely-to-be-automated

Best places to work:
http://fortune.com/best-companies/

Better decisions:
http://www.mckinsey.com/business-functions/strategy-and-corporate-finance/our-insights/strategic-principles-for-competing-in-the-digital-age

Big data:
https://hbr.org/2012/10/big-data-the-management-revolution

Big data: A retail gamechanger:
http://www.forbes.com/sites/bernardmarr/2015/11/10/big-data-a-game-changer-in-the-retail-sector/

Branding:
https://hbr.org/2010/12/branding-in-the-digital-age-youre-spending-your-money-in-all-the-wrong-places

CEO tenure:
http://fortune.com/2015/05/06/ceo-tenure-cisco/

Change v transformation:
https://www.linkedin.com/pulse/20140714023453-85816712-the-difference-between-change-and-transformation

Changing nature of work:
https://hbr.org/2013/12/the-peer-economy-will-transform-work-or-at-least-how-we-think-of-it

Co-bots:
https://www.ft.com/content/6d5d609e-02e2-11e6-af1d-c47326021344

Cognitive fitness:
https://hbr.org/2007/11/cognitive-fitness

Cognitive reserve:
https://www.weforum.org/agenda/2015/12/what-is-cognitive-reserve-and-how-do-we-increase-it/

Collective ambition:
https://hbr.org/2011/12/the-power-of-collective-ambition

Data capital:
https://www.technologyreview.com/s/601081/the-rise-of-data-capital/

Data driven business:
https://www-ssl.intel.com/content/www/us/en/big-data/building-a-data-driven-business.html

Death of a car salesman:
http://www.economist.com/news/business/21661656-no-one-much-likes-car-dealers-changing-system-will-be-hard-death-car-salesman

Decentralised leadership:
https://en.wikipedia.org/wiki/The_Starfish_and_the_Spider

Digital competition:
http://www.mckinsey.com/business-functions/strategy-and-corporate-finance/our-insights/strategic-principles-for-competing-in-the-digital-age

Digital defined:
http://www.mckinsey.com/industries/high-tech/our-insights/what-digital-really-means

Digital globalisation
https://hbr.org/2016/03/globalization-is-becoming-more-about-data-and-less-about-stuff

Digital leadership:
http://www.mckinsey.com/business-functions/digital-mckinsey/our-insights/adapting-your-board-to-the-digital-age

Digital strategy:
http://www.mckinsey.com/business-functions/strategy-and-corporate-finance/our-insights/the-economic-essentials-of-digital-strategy

Emerging markets middle class
http://www.ey.com/gl/en/issues/driving-growth/middle-class-growth-in-emerging-markets

Energy and natural resources:
http://www.mckinsey.com/mgi/our-research/natural-resources

Globalisation:
https://hbr.org/topic/globalization

Happiness and the hunter gatherer:
https://www.quora.com/Were-people-in-hunter-gatherer-societies-generally-happier-than-modern-people

Human organisation:
http://www.strategy-business.com/article/03309

Hunter gatherer economics:
https://www.quora.com/Which-economic-system-did-the-hunter-gatherer-societies-use

Hunter gatherer life:
http://www.h2g2.com/approved_entry/A2054675

Hunter gatherer to digital native:
http://information-revolutions.com/chapter01/

Incomplete leadership:
https://hbr.org/2007/02/in-praise-of-the-incomplete-leader

Intellectual capital:
http://www.telegraph.co.uk/business/2017/02/13/companies-failing-see-value-intellectual-property/

Internet of Things:
http://www.bain.com/publications/articles/internet-of-things-the-future-is-here-business-standard.aspx

Leadership guts:
https://www.goodreads.com/book/show/8017237-head-heart-and-guts

Leaderless organisations:
http://www.forbes.com/sites/drewhansen/2016/03/08/leaderless-management/

Managing talent in the digital age:
http://www.mckinsey.com/industries/high-tech/our-insights/managing-talent-in-a-digital-age

Marginal gains:
http://www.bbc.co.uk/sport/olympics/19174302

Motivation:
https://hbr.org/topic/motivating-people

http://www.ted.com/talks/dan_pink_on_motivation

Netflix: Reinventing HR:
https://hbr.org/2014/01/how-netflix-reinvented-hr

Oxford study on people entering workplace 50% robots
https://motherboard.vice.com/en_us/article/the-future-of-robot-labour-has-everything-to-do-with-capitalism

Product development:
http://tomtunguz.com/mckinseys-3-horizons/

Robots and marriage:
http://fortune.com/2016/12/26/human-robot-love-marriage-relationships/

Robots in the boardroom:
http://www.livemint.com/Consumer/zoYuqJV5VMA8XFcW5Nl3mO/Robots-in-the-boardroom-could-soon-be-a-reality-says-WEF-su.html

Sales transformation:
https://www.bcg.com/expertise/capabilities/marketing-sales/sales-channel-transformation.aspx

Satisfying work:
http://uk.businessinsider.com/malcolm-gladwell-on-great-jobs-satisfying-work-2014-11

Sense of purpose:
http://www.smartcompany.com.au/people-human-resources/leadership/34233-six-business-management-lessons-from-the-english-premier-league/

Servant leader:
https://hbr.org/2015/09/new-managers-need-a-philosophy-about-how-theyll-lead

Skills:
http://www.survivalinternational.org/articles/3380-tribal-conservation

Smart cities:
http://www.information-age.com/intelligent-streetlamps-and-intelligent-city-gartner-123458507/

Smart connected products:
https://hbr.org/2014/11/how-smart-connected-products-are-transforming-competition

Talent and leadership:
https://www.bcgperspectives.com/content/articles/leadership_talent_human_resources_global_leadership_talent_index/

Talent management:
http://futurestatetalent.com/ceos-prepare-for-talent-churn-in-the-digital-age/

Tesla strategy:
https://hbr.org/2015/05/teslas-new-strategy-is-over-100-years-old

The centre for collective intelligence:
http://cci.mit.edu/

The need for dreamers:
http://tompeters.com/pdfs/Tomato101804.pdf

Tom Peters - reimagine:
http://tompeters.com/pdfs/Tomato101804.pdf

Value creation:
https://www.greenbiz.com/blog/2013/03/26/why-disruptive-sustainability-new-leadership-framework

Virgin culture:
https://www.ukessays.com/essays/business/virgin-organizational-culture-and-history.php

Virgin: Talent attraction:
https://www.virgin.com/entrepreneur/richard-branson-how-to-attract-the-right-employees

Vision and purpose:
https://hbr.org/2014/09/your-companys-purpose-is-not-its-vision-mission-or-values

Wired: Long tail:
https://www.wired.com/2004/10/tail/

You can access the online references below, including the Amazon links to the books, by visiting:

www.ademccormack.com/digitalstrategy/biz-4/resources/

About the Author

Ade McCormack is focused on helping organisations thrive in the post-industrial world through the optimal engagement of people and judicious application of new technology.

Clients engage Ade when they need a 'zoom out' view of how the world is changing, followed by 'zoom in' guidance on how they can capitalise on these changes.

Ade has worked in over 30 countries, across many industries. Clients engage Ade in many ways including:

- Thought leader.
- Conference keynoter.
- Advisor and coach.

He is a former technologist, with a degree in Physics/Astrophysics.

Ade has written for several publications, including the Financial Times (circa 150 pieces). He has written several business books, including 'Beyond Nine to Five: Your career guide for the digital age'. He has also lectured at MIT Sloan School of Management on digital leadership.

Ade is married with one son. He enjoys martial arts, dancing and running. Running being his most effective form of self defence, closely followed by dancing.

Please turn over:

Website

www.ademccormack.com

Here you can explore a variety of resources, including Ade's blogs:

- Digital Life.
- Digital Strategy.

Connect

I would be delighted to connect with you on:

@ademccormack

LinkedIn: https://www.linkedin.com/in/ademccormack

69944004R00110

Made in the USA
Columbia, SC
30 April 2017